Unmasking: A Journey Through Fear to Embrace Reality

Unmasking: A Journey Through Fear to Embrace Reality

••••••••••••••••••••••••••••••

Jennifer Yah Legay

Copyright © 2025 by Jennifer Yah Legay
ISBN: Hardcover 1-979-8-218-55186-5

All rights reserved. No part of this book may be reproduced or transmitted in any form or by any means, electronic or mechanical, including photocopying, recording, or by any information storage and retrieval system, without permission in writing from the copyright owner.

This is a work of nonfiction. Names, people, places and incidents either are the product of the author's actual experience with people in her life, and any resemblance to any actual persons, living or dead, events, or locales is entirely coincidental.

This book was printed in the United States of America.

To order additional copies of this book, contact:
Clarke Publishing Communications & PBO, Inc
Tel. +336-602-1769
www.clarkepublish.com or www.amazon.com and www.jenniferlegay.com
contact: info@clarkepublish.com

Sales of this book without a front cover may be unauthorized. If this book is coverless, it may have been reported to the publisher as "unsold, or destroyed" and neither the author nor the publisher may have received payment for it.

Unmasking: A Journey Through Fear to Embrace Reality, is a work of nonfiction, references to all work of art, cities, counties, towns and villages, in Liberia and the United States of America are all real or factual. Names, Characters, incidents are the products of the author's direct experience.

2025 Clarke Publishing Communications & BPO, Inc.
Copyright © by Jennifer Yah Legay

All rights reserved
Published in the United States of America by Clarke Publishing Communications & BPO, Inc. Nonfiction Division, an imprint of Clarke Publishing Communications & BPO, Inc . 500 West 5th Street, Winston Salem, North Carolina 27101.

Cover designed by Albert Kizou
Cover photo taken from http://www.jenniferlegay.com

Printed in the United State of America
Published simultaneously in United States of America and globally.
https://www.clarkepulbish.com

Dedication

I would like to express my heartfelt gratitude to my audience and to everyone who supported me during my challenging times. To my wonderful daughters—Ernestine, Louise, Elaine, JoAnn—and my granddaughter Aya, I dedicate this moment to you all. Most importantly, I pay a special tribute to my late mother, Mrs. Tonia Greene Karyouwaye, whose acts of kindness have shaped me into the person I am today.

THANK YOU!

Author's Note

THIS BOOK IS based entirely on my life's events in Liberia and the United States of America. References to all works of art, cities, towns and villages in Liberia and cities in the United States of America are factual.

The key characters are all real people in Liberia and the Unted States of America, and a few actual Liberian government officials and warlords are mentioned.

Acknowledgments

I am deeply thankful to the Almighty God for bringing this dream to fruition by connecting me with my destiny helper throughout this journey. Words cannot adequately convey my gratitude to Dr. Emmanuel Clarke for his patience, guidance, and steadfast support during this process. Dr. Clarke is truly one of the most exceptional individuals in the publishing industry, and I am grateful to have had the opportunity to work alongside him. This endeavor would not have been possible without his invaluable assistance and guidance.

In honor of my late father, Mr. Jacob Nyan Legay, who believed it was essential to take me out of the village and send me to Monrovia for a modern education, I would like to express my gratitude for that difficult decision.

I would like to express my heartfelt gratitude to my beloved mother, Mrs. Yah Quaye Legay, who has consistently prayed for me since I left the village. She is not only my mother but also my steadfast prayer partner. Thank you, Mama.

PART I
THE YEARS OF INNOCENCE

CHAPTER 1

Who Am I

Nestled amidst rolling hills and expansive stretches of greenery, the village of Gipo (pronounced Geek-Po) presents a picturesque tableau on the canvas of Africa, specifically in Nimba County, Northeastern Liberia. Thatched-roof huts grace the landscape, their walls adorned with vibrant patterns that reflect the spirit of the villagers. Gipo serves as a sanctuary of community, where traditions are lovingly passed down through generations like cherished stories, and the heartbeat of the land resonates in every step. This is not only the place of my birth but also the birthplace of countless generations before me.

My name is Yah Tankehlay, which means *'the second daughter who dances.'* I was born into a polygamous family with 22 siblings, and I spent my formative years in this vibrant communal environment. Growing up in Gipo, I had two best friends, and together we thrived in our sleepy little town, surrounded by lush bushes and towering trees. Each day began with our journey to the family farm, followed by a group pilgrimage to the nearby creek to fetch water alongside other young people. The path we took was well-trodden, winding through tall grasses and beneath ancient baobab trees. As the first light of dawn illuminated the village, our silhouettes moved gracefully toward the water source. The creek, clear and babbling, held the secrets of Gipo's life. It was here that my worn calabash and sometimes clay jug met the cool, flowing stream, filling them with the essence of sustenance—water, of course.

The journey to the family farm seamlessly integrated into Gipo's daily rhythm. The fields, stretching beyond the village's forest, created a vibrant mosaic of crops, bathed in the golden glow of ripening rice under the sun. With a profound connection to the land, I would accompany my older siblings to inspect the traps we had set months before the rice plants began to sprout their seeds. During the growing season, the rice attracted groundhogs, bush rats, and other animals that feasted upon it. The farm was not merely a source of nourishment; it stood as a testament to my family's resilience and our deep-rooted relationship with the Earth.

As the sun sank beneath the village horizon, it painted the sky with a warm palette of colors, and Gipo surrendered to the enchanting embrace of the night. The village square, illuminated by the gentle glow of lanterns and the flickering flames of bonfires, transformed into a vibrant stage for the evening's festivities. I earned the name Tankehlay, a tribute to my deep love and passion for dance during my childhood. Under the silvery moonlight, the villagers gathered, and the rhythmic pulse of drums echoed through the cool night air.

Beneath the enchanting moonlight, I would partake in the dance that intertwined Gipo's past with its present. Dressed in vibrant fabrics, the women and girls of the village moved in harmonious celebration of life, laughter, and love. The moon, a silent observer of countless gatherings, cast its silvery glow upon the dancers. The night filled with laughter, the crackling of bonfires, and the vibrant energy of communal unity.

My movements beneath the moonlight mirrored the spirit of Gipo—resilient, intertwined with nature, and deeply anchored in our Mano tradition. The dance transcended mere physical expression; it became a shared language that conveyed our Mano heritage, gratitude, and the enduring connection between the villagers and their beloved village, Gipo.

How can I forget the roads I have traveled and the sacred conversations my young ears have heard? Why would I not remember the ancient myths of dragons and dwarfs believed to lurk in the forests of Gipo? How can I regret the troubled times that prepared me for the successful life I now enjoy and appreciate? Without a shred of doubt, I can confidently say that God has truly blessed me. I am a single mother of four beautiful daughters, a grandmother, a Master of Science graduate from East Tennessee State University, a Board-Certified Family Nurse Practitioner, and the proud owner of a beautiful home valued at over half a million dollars. I am also a woman of great faith. In retrospect, I have no regrets; instead, I am thankful for all that has transpired. My journey is just beginning as I embark on a new mission to empower women around the world.

As a child in Gipo, I thought it was the best place in the world. Gipo was beautiful and welcoming to locals, but mysterious to outsiders. My childhood was special, especially growing up in a home with many wives of our father. At home, the women prepared food together. We the kids shared clothes, and slept in the same area based on our gender—boys crowded in one room, so did the girls. Even though I joined the family later, I was fascinated by stories of life before I was born. I heard how peaceful it was among the women living with our father. They shared chores, took care of each other's children, and spent time with our father without fighting, even if there were feelings of jealousy. Our father sent all his children to the village school for elementary education. I loved the village school because I learned the alphabet through songs and did math. I enjoyed this life until I was about 10 years old, according to my parents' guess since they weren't educated. While many Western societies may not approve of polygamy and inherited wives, this was part of my culture and my early life until I moved to the capital city, Monrovia.

For a 10-year-old child, leaving the comfort of the village where I had everything that brought me joy and moving to the city was a blend of excitement and trepidation. It was exhilarating because it felt like a dream realized. However, it also turned my life upside down, as the familiar world I cherished was being replaced by the unknown, leaving me feeling profoundly sad and frightened. If given the choice between remaining in Gipo and relocating to Monrovia, I would have chosen the latter, for it represented everything I aspired to be. By the time I reached 10, Gipo was ingrained in my very being.

Unmasking: A Journey Through Fear to Embrace Reality

In contrast, the City of Monrovia was an obsession for many of us in the village. Whenever someone returned from Monrovia, we would eagerly gather around to hear them speak English and admire their radiant skin and fashionable clothes. To us, the people from Monrovia seemed superior and distinct from those of us who lived in Gipo. Each night, I would pray for the opportunity to one day visit Monrovia. Despite my youthful prayers and daydreams, I cherished every moment spent with my family and friends in our little haven, rich with myths and legends.

As a child growing up in Gipo, I became familiar with the activities of my family members at home. However, as I grew older, most of my father's wives had departed. By the time I turned ten, I had only encountered two of the seven women my father had married. These were my mother and a young woman who was believed to be my father's last wife. My mother informed me that two of the women had passed away when I was around five years old. One of his wives returned to her family after a divorce, while the other two left my father and remarried by the time I reached seven. As you can see, I come from a very large family with several dozen siblings, many of whom I do not know, particularly those children my father had outside of his marriage. Below are some names of my brothers and sisters:

These are the names of children born by my mother: Saye Nentoh Legay (deceased), Kou Legay, Nyan Legay (deceased), Paye Legay (deceased),

Jennifer Yah Legay

Stephen Dakar Wuo Legay, Josephine Yei Legay. Here are the names of my other siblings from the other mothers: James Paye Legay (deceased) a son of my father's inherited wife, Dorothy Kou Legay (the mother of the family), Priscilla Yar Legay, Stanley Saye Legay (deceased), John Nyan Legay (deceased), Cooper Saye Legay, Yei Legay, Marie Nohn Legay, Tenneh Kou Legay, Lemeo Nyan Legay (deceased), Yei Joyce Legay, Patricia Yar Legay, Spencer Paye Legay, Angeline Yar Legay, Morris Paye Legay, Berta Fohnia Legay, Saye Yeigbeh Legay, Kouyoungwee Legay, Saye Koogbeh Legay, Saye Junior Legay, Nohngbei Legay.

On the topic of inherited wife within our Mano Culture, a son may marry one or all of his father's wives. This can only be done when the father dies. This was the case with my own mother, she was inherited by my older brother, James Legay, who came from another mother. He inherited my mother after my father's death. That relationship produced a child which is my little sister. The practice of a son marrying or inheriting his father's wife after the death of the father is prevalent among many tribes in Africa. Two of my father's wives were inherited wives from his own father who is our grandfather.

Growing up in the village, my friends and I were very close and interacted well with one another. Among the three of us, I was the best cultural dancer. My talent for dancing at such a young age earned me the nickname Tankehlay, which means 'dancing woman' or 'dancer' in the Mano dialect. My mother told me that I began dancing as a toddler. Whenever

Unmasking: A Journey Through Fear to Embrace Reality

I heard the beat of a drum or any musical instrument, I would jump up and down in her lap with excitement. Even when I was playing on the ground, I would move my body back and forth rhythmically, mimicking a dance. As I grew older, the moment I heard the sound of a drum, I would stop whatever I was doing and rush to join the music. My mom mentioned that people enjoyed watching me dance, as I was often invited to participate in village plays and events. Despite being younger than everyone else in the group, I was allowed to take the lead as a dancer. I fondly remember performing and receiving coins from the audience for my dance moves. I would use that money to buy candy and Kala, a round doughnut made of cream of rice, and sometimes flour.

During my childhood in Gipo, I was affectionately known as Yah Tankehlay, a name that still resonates with people today. I danced throughout my time in the village, and my friends and I would gather outside in the late evening under the moonlight, playing until we were exhausted. We often collected old cups, empty gallons, and anything we could use as makeshift musical instruments to create traditional music. Once we began to play, a crowd would gather to watch us sing and dance. Our performances not only entertained but also earned us candy money, as audience members would throw coins in appreciation of our talent.

As children, we established our own routine in the village. During the day, we would visit the Wehyee River, the main river in the area, to bathe and wash our clothes. We enjoyed playing water tag and frolicking in the beautiful brown and white sand along the riverbank. To avoid upsetting our parents when they returned home from the farm, we made sure to collect enough drinking water and bath water for our households during the late afternoon hours, especially on days when we didn't accompany them to the farm. In Gipo, the older adults looked out for the children, fostering a strong sense of community.

As children, we were captivated by the tale of the Wehyee River and its significance in our village's history. We learned that people discovered babies along the riverbank, and the village legend spoke of men and women emerging from the river at night to join the villagers during celebrations. Whenever the community gathered to play music and dance under the stars, the water people would appear. However, as dawn approached, they would swiftly retreat into the river, vanishing from sight. We believed these stories were mere fairy tales, delighting in the joy they brought us. Yet, sometimes, the most pleasurable aspects of life can lead to our downfall. My friends and I bathed and washed our clothes in that ominous river, even drinking its water from various spots around the village. All of these experiences occurred during my innocent years in Gipo.

I was uncertain about the spiritual implications of my activities in my place of birth and the beliefs my family held. As Thomas Jefferson once remarked, *"Ignorance of the law is no excuse in any country. If it were so, the laws would lose their effect, because it can always be pretended."* This principle seems to

Unmasking: A Journey Through Fear to Embrace Reality

extend to spiritual matters as well. Multiple scriptures in the Bible (Deuteronomy 5:9, Exodus 34:7, Numbers 14:18, Psalm 109:14, Isaiah 65:6-7) illustrate that being unaware of generational or foundational curses does not exempt one from their consequences. Recently, while working on this book, I engaged in a conversation with one of my uncles, a knowledgeable historian with deep insights about our village, Gipo. He shared stories about life in the village during his youth, and our discussion became quite captivating, lasting nearly two hours. During our conversation, he remarked, *"Your father was a great man."* This piqued my curiosity, prompting me to ask what made my father so esteemed. He explained, *"Your father was well-respected in the village, and at one point, the entire community came together to elect him as the village president. They constructed a hut with stairs leading up to a magnificent tree at the village entrance. During the Christmas and New Year seasons, the men organized a celebration where they would carry your father in a hammock from his home, hoisting him on their shoulders while the entire village—men, women, and children—sang as they walked toward the treehouse. They would ensure that his feet never touched the ground. Upon reaching the treehouse, they would ascend the stairs and place him inside. He would sit in that tree while the villagers danced and sang praises to him as if he were a king or a god."* He described this event as a week-long celebration, a truly beautiful occasion. It was the first time I had heard such a remarkable yet unsettling story about my family. I was struck with shock and fear as I grasped the spiritual implications of his words. The realization that my father was not only an idol worshipper but also the idol himself was frightening. My village was far removed from Christianity, with not a single church in Gipo.

Reflecting on my past, I have come to realize that idol worship, incest, and witchcraft practices were, and continue to be, common in Gipo. One prevalent practice among my people that I observed as a child was necromancy, or communication with the dead or demons from the dark world. Growing up in the village, my parents worked tirelessly to cultivate our farms each year for our livelihood. They would clear the underbrush, cut down trees, and fell large timber with machetes and axes at the start of the farming season. Although this was a lengthy process carried out in stages, I found joy in watching it unfold, as it deepened my appreciation for the fruits of their labor. The farming I witnessed was hard labor subsistence farming, focused solely on producing food for our consumption. Lacking the necessary tools, my parents invested immense effort to complete their farming tasks. A single family could not manage this labor alone, so the villagers devised a cooperative system known as the Coup. Members of the Coup would rotate from farm to farm, assisting each other by clearing bushes, cutting down trees, and sometimes burning debris. This rotation continued until every member's plot was prepared for planting.

Families without representation in the group had to pay Coup members to perform the work on their behalf. Typically, each family was responsible for burning the cleared bushes once the land was ready. The cycle would then begin anew, as they cleared the remnants of burnt trees, removing stumps and roots in preparation for planting crops. When the planting season arrived, the women would gather to sow rice seeds and other crops on each Coup member's farm. This spirit of teamwork persisted until the harvest season, which was my favorite time in Gipo, as we enjoyed the fresh rice from the fields, which smelled and tasted delightful. As my father was the village leader, he oversaw all aspects of crop production on his farm. I rarely saw him working alongside the group; he was liken to a king, offering the Coup members tokens of appreciation for their efforts in clearing, burning, and maintaining his farm.

Whenever my parents had a group working for them, they would prepare delicious meals. However, before the group arrived to eat, or even before we could savor the food ourselves, my mother would take a portion, mix it with palm oil, and carry it to the intersection of the road leading to the farm. There, she would place it at the entrance of the farm on a specific type of leaf as an offering to the gods of harvest, whom they believed to be their deceased family members or ancestors. She would call out the names of all the departed family members and relatives, informing them that she had brought their food, and she would ask for their blessings on the farm. This ritual was performed annually at all stages of the farming process. In Gipo, cooperation prevailed over competition.

Several years after leaving Gipo and growing up in Monrovia, I discovered that my father was involved with a highly secretive society known as Gbon. During a conversation with my mother, she revealed that my father had introduced this society to the village of Gipo, actively encouraging and recruiting others to join in this idol worship. As a child, I recalled the gatherings of men at my father's compound, which occurred from time to time. Sometimes, these gatherings would be quite large, and I noticed that no women were present among them. People traveled from all corners of the region for what resembled a conference. During these events, the women would prepare large quantities of food, while musicians entertained with a variety of beautiful instruments. It appeared to be a festive occasion, and I was blissfully unaware of the darker activities taking place behind the scenes. Unbeknownst to me, I consumed food and drank water that had been sacrificed to the many idol gods worshipped by the people of Gipo. I danced to the rhythms of idol music in the presence of worshippers, especially during their rituals held under the Palava hut in my father's compound. They would beat large drums, play various musical instruments, and chant openly, encouraging others to join their cult. After the public displays of worship, they would retreat to a small Palava hut, devoid of windows, to perform the remainder of their rituals in secrecy, accessible only to cult members. All of this transpired within my father's compound.

My family, particularly my father, was a staunch idol worshiper, a fact I only came to realize as I matured and embraced Christianity in Monrovia. I would have never imagined that my father could be a servant of the devil. Whenever I looked at him, I saw a tall, handsome man with a rich chocolate complexion, a golden tooth gleaming in his smile, which had the power to illuminate any room. I often pondered how such an attractive man could serve an unknown god. I believe some of my siblings perceived him in the same light. I sometimes wonder if my father was even aware of his involvement in satanic practices. During his tenure as the village chief, he was known to be kindhearted and courageous, a figure whom everyone respected for guidance. My father was not only cherished for his leadership as the village chief but also for his commitment to educating girls. I learned that many women from Gipo and surrounding towns received an education thanks to his efforts. In his role as chief, he encouraged villagers to send their daughters to school at a time when many believed that women should not be educated. He even supported girls whose families could not afford school fees. My father's passion for girls' education was evident. Despite lacking formal education himself, he dedicated himself to ensuring that all his daughters left the village to pursue their studies. Only those who were unwilling to attend or faced mistreatment returned home without an education. Although I had longed to go to Monrovia, when the moment arrived, chaos ensued—I found myself reluctant to leave Gipo.

This is how it all began, as far as I can remember. One early morning, my father instructed my mother to prepare me for a journey to Monrovia with two of his friends who were traveling to the city on a business trip. I distinctly recall that it was a Thursday, Ganta City's Market Day, when many cars would head to the village to transport businesspeople to Ganta, the largest city in Nimba County. I didn't know the month or the year until later, when I was in Monrovia and learned it was May of 1983.

That morning, while I was in the room with my mother, searching for clothes to wear, I noticed tears in her eyes. She said to me, *"My daughter, listen to the people you're going to. Don't be hardheaded; do what they tell you. You are going far from us, and you don't know these people, so be respectful."* Meanwhile, my father was outside the house, calling for my mother, *"Yar Yorgbo, bring the girl! The people are ready to go!"*

I quickly got ready, donning my best dress, a navy-blue Christmas dress from the previous year. It had an elastic band just above my belly button, but I had worn it so often that the thread had loosened under my right arm, leaving a tear down the side. There was no time to fix it, so I held onto the torn side of my dress as I stepped outside.

As I approached my father, I saw the two men standing beside him. He said, *"These men will take you to your sister Dorothy in Monrovia. I want you to go to school and become a civilized woman."* Still clutching the torn part of my dress, I turned to my mother and saw tears streaming down her cheeks. I reached out, wrapped my little arms around her thighs, and held her tightly as we both cried for a moment. But my father insisted I not delay his friends any longer. He yelled, *"The people have to go! Get in the car!"*

Frightened, I hurriedly climbed into the car, squeezing myself between my father's friends in the back seat. Since this was a business trip according to my father, I sat silently between the two strangers for the entire journey. Other passengers were also in the vehicle, heading either to Monrovia or Ganta. Being so small and wedged between those two tall men, I could hardly see outside the car windows for a clear view of the world beyond.

As we drove away from Gipo that morning, I could only imagine the tears streaming down my mother's cheeks. The driver skillfully maneuvered the vehicle from the village road onto the main route leading to Ganta, and I leaned sideways, eager to catch a glimpse of the road ahead. Along the way, I observed a mix of beautiful houses and makeshift dwellings. The journey from Gipo to Ganta was marked by unpaved, dusty roads. Upon our arrival in Ganta, it was nearly noon, with the sun positioned high in the sky. The streets were bustling with activity, thanks to the open-air market, where vendors showcased an array of beautiful goods. After dropping off the businesspeople, the driver continued to the Monrovia Parking Station. We disembarked, and I followed the two men as they sought a vehicle to take us to Monrovia. Within a few minutes, they discovered a smaller car ready to transport us to our destination. At that time, I was unfamiliar with the names of cars as I am now, but I found the little car to be quite charming, with seats that were far more comfortable than those of the vehicle that had brought us from the village to Ganta City. As we traveled, I could see the scenery outside more clearly, without the need to crane my neck.

The journey from Gipo to Monrovia typically takes about five hours or less; however, for me, it felt like an all-day ride. Throughout the trip, my father's friends were exceptionally kind. They offered me food and frequently asked, "Are you okay?" While I was fine, I couldn't shake the feeling of unease around the two unfamiliar men. A sense of fear gripped me, as I worried about whether I would ever see my mother again. Each time we approached a security checkpoint and I noticed someone in police or security uniform approaching our car, I would instinctively shrink back in fear, convinced they were coming to take me away. The officer would converse with the driver, and we would be allowed to pass through the checkpoint. I struggled to comprehend their words, as they spoke in hushed tones, and my understanding of English was limited.

After what felt like an eternity, we finally arrived in Monrovia as the sun dipped below the horizon of the Atlantic Ocean. At that moment, I realized I was in a completely different world. Lights adorned the poles everywhere, and people strolled along the roadside as cars whizzed by. *"This place is really fine ooooh,"* I whispered to myself in Mano. While I was captivated by the city's beauty, thoughts of my mother and my best friends back in Gipo lingered in my mind. I wished they could share this moment with me. The lights, the cars, the buildings—all of them were breathtaking to me. Clutching my dress with one hand and a plastic bag containing the rest of my clothes in the other, I stepped out of the car alongside the men, making our way to my sister's house across the street. Sensing our arrival, everyone emerged from her house to greet us. She exchanged a few words with the men before they entrusted me to her care.

Sister Dorothy and her younger sister Yei are two of my half-sisters from one of my father's other wives. It was my first time meeting both of them. They welcomed me into their home, and Yei offered me some food, which I found delicious. After eating, she suggested I take a shower before going to bed. This was a new experience for me; I was accustomed to bathing in a bucket or in the Wehyee River. However, here I was, witnessing water streaming from the wall above me through the showerhead. It felt intimidating, but Yei reassured me that it wouldn't hurt. That night, I took a shower, holding my breath in fear with every passing second, yet I emerged unscathed, just as Yei had promised. At that time, my sister lived in Jallah Town, located in the southwest part of Monrovia. My first encounter with city life was unforgettable. I was relieved not to have to pour water over my shoulders from a bucket or travel to the river for a bath. The days and weeks I spent with my sister in Jallah Town were extraordinary for me as a newcomer to the city. I was now eating with a spoon instead of my hands, and we cooked on charcoal in a metal stove rather than using blazing firewood positioned between rocks. I believed I would stay with my sister forever, as our father had indicated, but I was mistaken; my journey to the city was leading me elsewhere. At my sister's house, I enjoyed the streetlights and the constant flow of cars passing by both day and night.

One quiet day, while sitting in a chair in the room, my sister informed me that I had been brought to Monrovia to help care for someone's baby as a domestic servant. Hearing this was not pleasant; I had been led to believe that I was coming to live with my sister Dorothy in Monrovia. Yet, sometimes the path to greatness takes unexpected turns. The woman who would later become my foster mother had a baby in January of 1983. She asked one of her friends, Maima, to find a little girl who could assist her with her child. Maima then reached out to my sister Dorothy to see if she knew of a girl who could help her friend. Prior to this, my father had been urging my sister Dorothy to bring me from the village, as I was his only daughter still living there. He wanted me to leave the village and move to the city so that I could attend school and receive an education. At that time, I learned that my father was suffering from a life-limiting illness, and it seemed he understood that he might not survive. In hindsight, this could explain his urgency in wanting me out of the village before his passing. I was told that he frequently pressed my sister to get me out of Gipo. Unbeknownst to me, my father was battling a terminal illness that would ultimately take his life. All I can say is that my transition from the village to Monrovia was a divine intervention.

CHAPTER 2

LIFE IN MONROVIA

As I acclimated to my new home in Jallah Town, my life was unexpectedly turned upside down. I was uprooted and placed in a different household with a family that felt strange and unfamiliar. This situation posed a significant challenge for me as a 10-year-old child, who had been forcibly separated from my mother by a father pursuing his own agenda for his children. I felt confused and frightened. Having only spent two and a half weeks at my sister's house, I struggled to fit in with the others. I experienced feelings of loneliness, rejection from my own sister, and disappointment due to my parents' actions. Jallah Town, while not the most desirable area of Monrovia, held great significance for me as it was a vast improvement over my previous living conditions. The contrast between Jallah Town and Gipo was striking. Jallah Town was urban, bustling with a diverse array of people from various ethnic backgrounds, communicating in multiple dialects and English, unlike Gipo, where everyone spoke Mano. In Jallah Town, I slept in a bed rather than on a mat spread across a mud floor. I enjoyed three hearty meals a day, sitting at a table instead of on the ground as I had in Gipo.

Upon my arrival in Monrovia, I quickly developed an affection for the bustling neighborhood and the vibrant shanty houses nearby, where the residents appeared content with their lives. Many of the inhabitants of Jallah Town were impoverished individuals navigating a city heavily monitored by men in military uniforms wielding American-made M16 rifles and other firearms. Despite the grim atmosphere, I found myself increasingly enamored with my new community. The children in the house shared with me that the President, a military figure, resides on Capitol Hill, not far from our home. They told me that every December, he gathers all the little children at his residence, the Executive Mansion, to host a Christmas party for them. During this festive occasion, he generously distributes gifts filled with toys, candy, and various ornaments. As I learned that I would be leaving this vibrant utopia, overshadowed by Liberia's oldest institution of higher learning, the University of Liberia, I felt a deep sense of heartbreak. I truly wished to remain in Jallah Town!

Often, our destination in life is not necessarily what we envision or believe is best for us. Despite the uncertainties we face on our journey, it is what God has ordained for us, allowing Him to be glorified through our successes. God's plan for an individual's life does not imply a life of ease, where one rides on a white horse from birth or dines from a silver platter. I vividly remember that it was two and a half weeks after I arrived at my sister's home in Jallah Town, Monrovia, around 7:00 PM, when my sister Dorothy returned from work accompanied by another woman. I felt as though I had been struck in the gut when she informed me that I would be leaving the house for another location. The woman, whom I later learned was Sister Maima, was my sister's best friend. She had asked my sister to allow me to help babysit one of her friend's newborns. Much like the situation in Gipo, I was reluctant to go. However, I lacked the willpower to resist or escape. Remembering my mother's advice, I had come to Monrovia to pursue an education that she never had the opportunity to attain. I needed to be strong to make both my mother and father proud.

My sister instructed me, *"Go into the room and pack your clothes. You will be leaving to live with one of our friends, and I will visit you often to check on you."* I hurriedly ran to the room to gather the few clothes I had. That evening, my sister arranged for a taxicab that took us all to the Township of Barnesville, located about 25 to 30 miles outside of Monrovia. Barnesville is one of Monrovia's suburbs. After several minutes in the vehicle, crossing over two bridges, we finally arrived at the house. Having grown accustomed to the bright and sometimes dazzling streetlights in Jallah Town, I was struck by how dark the surroundings were. *"Oh my God, I am back in another Gipo,"* I thought to myself. *"How could I have come from the well-lit Jallah Town back to a dark Gipo, albeit with a different name, Barnesville?"* I whispered to myself. On our way to Barnesville, we navigated unpaved, dusty roads filled with potholes. The road reminded me of our journey from Gipo to Ganta, which also featured an unpaved, pothole-ridden path and a two-lane highway.

For reasons I couldn't quite grasp, I felt a profound sense of unhappiness as I stepped into my new home. The house, a spacious five-bedroom dwelling, was enveloped by lush mango trees and dense brush. It was home to several family members, yet the atmosphere felt heavy. Perhaps my discontent stemmed from the house's resemblance to my father's compound in the village. Upon entering, I heard Maima calling out a name, *"Tonia,"* followed by a flurry of English words that eluded my understanding. I gathered she was saying something like, *"your daughter, or the girl is here."* She then engaged in a conversation with a woman who would later be introduced to me as my foster mother. During their exchange, I felt lost; my grasp of English was limited, and my conversational skills were even more so—everything they said seemed to drift over my head. Once I was settled, Maima and my sister concluded their visit. Just before my sister departed, she approached me where I sat and spoke in our Mano dialect, saying, *"This is your mother now; this is where you will be from now on. Don't give the people a hard time. I will return to check on you. I want you to stay here, focus, and learn something that will help you become someone important in the future. Remember, everything will be okay. You are not alone."* As I heard those words, hot tears streamed down my cheeks. In that moment, I recalled my mother's final words to me before I left Gipo: *"You are going far from us, and you don't know the people, so be respectful."*

I was initially unfamiliar with the people around me, and they, in turn, did not know me. The language barrier posed a challenge, as I struggled to comprehend their spoken English, and they found it difficult to understand my dialect. However, their willingness to embrace me made the adjustment process far easier than I had anticipated. This experience taught me that love can make anything possible. My foster mother was a God-fearing and kind-hearted woman. Despite the challenges in understanding her at times, she dedicated herself to helping me improve my English skills. Just as a man can transform a woman's perceived flaws into beauty through love, my foster mother and her family did the same for me. She guided me in becoming a decent young woman, a loving and humble wife, and a nurturing mother to my children. I lived in that home with my foster mother and her family from 1983 until my marriage in December 1998.

Reflecting on my past, my journey from Jallah Town to Barnesville was truly remarkable and a significant learning experience. On my first night at our house in Barnesville, I shared a room and a bed with Gama. The next morning, I awoke to a stark contrast; unlike my sister's place in Jallah Town, there were no cars passing by. Instead, the yard of my new family was bustling with human traffic. It was ideally situated along a footpath frequented by people heading to town, schools, or the market to shop for food. This thoroughfare ensured that our yard was always lively with activity.

Sister Tonia, whom I affectionately called my foster mother, took the time to introduce me to everyone who passed through our yard. One of the key factors that helped me adapt quickly to my new environment was Sister Tonia's approach. She treated me as she would any other child in the home, communicating with me as if I fully understood her. This encouragement allowed me to start attending school right at the beginning of the new school year. Within just 1-2 months, I had acclimatized and was conversing in English quite well. Although I occasionally mixed Mano and English when I struggled to find the right words, I was never shy about it. I engaged in conversations when necessary and refused to let anyone take advantage of me due to my imperfect English.

At home, I had two cousins, Gama and Faith, who were around my age. We spent a lot of time together, playing, arguing over our differences, and even fighting when we felt someone was being taken advantage of. During my initial weeks, when we had more free time, Gama would perform for me, singing, dancing, and explaining her words, though I often struggled to understand her. I believe she was trying to entertain me, but I would respond in Mano, saying, *"I don't understand what you're saying."* This became our routine until I began to learn a bit of English. There were days when Gama and I took turns washing the dishes. Our kitchen was outdoors, where we cooked over firewood, unlike my sister's house in Jallah Town, which used charcoal. Cooking with firewood brought back memories of Gipo, the village I longed for.

I recall a particular day when our mother prepared Palm Butter soup. After we shared the meal, only a small amount of soup remained in the pot. Before adding water to wash it, I decided to savor the remnants by licking the sides and bottom of the pot. To enjoy every last bit of sauce, I would rub my finger along the pot and then lick the soup off my finger. It was clear that Gama also desired the soup, but rather than asking me to share, she chose to snatch the pot from my hands. In response, I quickly reclaimed the pot, and in the heat of the moment, she struck my arm. Without hesitation, I retaliated. Before I knew it, we were embroiled in a tussle over the soup pot. During the scuffle, she bit my hand, prompting me to yell out. My cries attracted the attention of everyone in the house and yard. Soon, my foster mother and several family members rushed out to separate us. Once we were pulled apart, we were asked to recount what had transpired. Gama shared her version of the story, but when it was my turn, all I could manage to say was, 'her tooth in Mano,' pointing to the bite mark on my hand. In our Mano dialect, I kept repeating, '*Ai Sohn*,' which means '*her teeth.*' At that time, I understood English better than I could speak it. I heard my mother say, '*You know you can't speak English, yet you want to fight. You both can leave, but I don't want to see or hear about any more fighting.*' After being dismissed by our mother, Gama and I became the best of friends and sisters. We would argue occasionally, but we never fought again until we grew up, I got married, and left the family home.

Once I became comfortable and started attending school, I found myself reluctant to return to Gipo. In fact, the memories of Gipo began to fade as I grew to love my life in Barnesville. I also developed a passion for school. I often reminded myself that it was education that brought me to Monrovia to be with my sister. In Barnesville, I attended Barnesville Public School, a quaint elementary school situated along the road leading to Dixville. To reach the school from Barnesville Oldfield, we had to navigate a narrow footpath through the bushes, crossing a creek or swamp that sometimes overflowed its banks during the rainy season. When the water rose, we would often have to remove our shoes, and at times, even our clothes, to make our way to and from school. The school's principal, Teacher Washington, was a strict disciplinarian. Students were required to arrive early and line up for devotion before the flag was raised. If a student was late and missed the flag hoisting, they would face punishment in front of the entire school during devotion the following day. During this physical punishment, Mr. Washington would ask the student, *"Why are you being whipped?"*

On days when I was late, I would run as fast as I could to avoid punishment and embarrassment, hoping to arrive before the flag went up. One day, believing I was late, I spotted a man on the other side of the creek bending down to tie his shoes. Without thinking, I jumped into the water and dashed across without checking who it was. To my shock, it was our principal, Teacher Washington. That day turned out to be one of the worst of my life. Passing by him without stopping or slowing down was a grave mistake for any student, and it was particularly regrettable for me. Although he refrained from whipping me as he usually would, he humiliated me in front of the entire school during devotion, calling me all sorts of names. He labeled me as stupid, rude, and undisciplined, explaining to the other students that I had nearly pushed him into the water. He jokingly remarked that I almost baptized him that morning as I rushed past him. He didn't stop there; later that evening, he came to our house to inform my parents of the incident. From that day on, he referred to me as a '*Bad Girl*' whenever he saw me at school. The other students began to tease me and call me names just like he did. It was humiliating, but I refused to let their taunts deter me from my education. I was determined to learn, to gain an education, and to become someone of significance. I understood that if I allowed the principal and my peers to discourage me from attending school, I would miss the very reason I was sent to Monrovia. Had I chosen to stop going to school and return to Gipo, I would have missed out on the knowledge my father intended for me to acquire in Monrovia. I persevered, continued my studies, and even achieved a double promotion that school year, despite the shame and humiliation. While many of my friends considered me smart, I believed I was simply blessed to retain everything the teacher taught us in class.

During the dry season in Liberia, my foster family produced red palm oil. As children, we were entrusted with the responsibility of venturing into the bushes after school to gather palm nuts that had been cut down by my mother's cousin, Joseph Greene, or by someone she had hired for the task. Our job was to transport these nuts to another location for palm oil production. After school, we would return home to change our clothes in preparation for the task of collecting the palm nuts. Often, when we arrived home, the food was not yet ready, and we sometimes had only one meal a day. To kick off our work, we would often find dry Gari— a creamy-white granular flour with a slightly fermented flavor and sour taste, produced from cassava tubers and typically eaten as a main meal with soup or stew— along with some sugar to sustain us before heading into the bush. This routine became a staple for us throughout the dry season in Liberia, and it was a challenging endeavor for me. I often found myself questioning whether I was in Monrovia or somewhere in Gipo. Life with my foster parents felt strikingly similar to life in Gipo. We would venture into the bushes to gather firewood, just as we did in the village. I observed women fishing with their nets, reminiscent of the women in Gipo. However, one significant difference was that my new family was a Christian family, which I cherished. At home, we held devotion every Sunday morning and attended church services each week. I participated in Sunday School and the children's choir, and as I grew into young womanhood, I continued to serve and nurture my belief in God.

In the previous chapter, I recounted how my father was suffering from an illness when he sent me to Monrovia, and he passed away just a few months after my arrival. My siblings from various parts of Liberia, including Monrovia, attended his funeral in Gipo, but I was not among them. I mourned my father's death for several weeks, often retreating behind the house to cry and refusing to eat. My foster mother informed my sister Dorothy about my persistent tears and my refusal to eat. In response, sister Dorothy promised to come and take me to see my mother, but she never followed through. After a period of mourning and not seeing any family members, I eventually decided to move on and found happiness again.

A couple of years after my father's death, I heard that my mother began to inquire about my whereabouts, as I had not attended his funeral in Gipo. She was worried that something might have happened to me, but sister Dorothy was reluctant to share the truth. This situation created a complex emotional tension between my sister and my mother. With the help of some elderly family members, sister Dorothy eventually brought my mother to Monrovia to see where I lived. One evening, while I was away at choir practice, sister Dorothy dropped my mother off at my foster home. Unbeknownst to me, my mother was in the house, and my foster mother was likely trying to surprise me by keeping it a secret. That evening, as I walked back from choir practice with a few friends, we were discussing the songs we had practiced. Suddenly, I heard my mother call out to me, "*neilay*" (which means '*children's mother*' in Mano)—a name only she used for me. The yard was dimly lit by a single bulb hanging near the back door, where a bamboo reed bench was positioned against the wall. I paused mid-conversation, thinking I had imagined the sound. I told myself it couldn't be my mother, as there was no way she could be here. After a brief silence, she called out again, "*neilay maleh*" (meaning '*children's mother, that's me*'). I ran to her and leaped into her arms, and everyone around us burst into laughter. We embraced for a moment, but then she began to cry, saying, *"Your father is no more."* Although we cried together, seeing her brought me immense joy, making me feel as if I were back in Gipo. After a moment of shared sorrow, I asked about my friends, only to learn that they had moved on to live with others for school. My mother stayed with us for a week, a week filled with joy and the rekindling of our bond. I wished for her to stay longer, but ultimately, that was beyond my control.

I felt a deep sense of loss when my mother left to return to Gipo. In my longing to be with her, I became increasingly stubborn at home. I resorted to any behavior that might compel my foster mother to send me back to Gipo. This was especially true when my sister Dorothy warned me that she would send me back if I caused any trouble. My defiance grew; I was determined to return to Gipo. I tried everything to provoke my foster mother into sending me back, but she remained resolute. The tipping point came when I dumped Walker's food in the rain. I had prepared the family meal that day and shared it as I usually did, but an argument erupted between Walker and me. Although I can't recall the specifics, my foster mother intervened, urging me to stop, but I ignored her. In a fit of anger, I seized Walker's food and threw it outside. That act was the last straw for my foster mother—she had reached her limit with my rebelliousness. The following day, I found myself on a bus heading to my sister Dorothy, who had moved to Saye Town, adjacent to Jallah Town. Although I never intended to hurt my foster mother's feelings, I refrained from apologizing, fearing it would hinder my chances of going to Gipo to be with my mother. When I arrived at my sister Dorothy's house, she was still at work. Upon returning home that evening and finding me there, she said, *"I've told you that I don't have a place for you here, so I will send you with whoever is going to Gipo as soon as I can."* Shortly after, my late brother, Mr. James Paye Legay, was traveling to Gipo in his personal vehicle. Sister Dorothy asked him to take me along, and I gladly accepted. Upon our arrival in Gipo, he greeted my mother with the words, *"Your daughter has rejected civilization and has come to work the farms; here she is."*

At that time, no one was pleased with my decision to return to Gipo—not even my biological mother, whom I longed for. She was unaware of my return, and I could see her disappointment etched on her face. Unlike the warm welcome and embrace I received during her visit to Monrovia, this time was different. Instead, she urged me to prepare for the coup, insisting that I contribute to the family's farming efforts. Although she was upset with Sister Dorothy for not bringing me back to Gipo with the other children for my father's burial, she still did not want me to live there again. All she wanted was to know that I was alive and well. Reflecting on it now, I believe her visit to Monrovia may have been a mistake; it awakened a deep maternal longing within me that led to my rebellious behavior after she left.

Around the same time I arrived in Gipo, one of my mother's nieces, Oretha, gave birth to a baby boy in

Ganta in September 1986 via cesarean delivery. After a couple of weeks in Gipo, my cousin's mother asked my mother if I could go to Ganta to help her daughter care for the baby for a few weeks. While in Ganta, the baby's mother began experiencing complications, which were attributed to the surgery. Consequently, she was taken to the hospital and readmitted. I was left with her boyfriend and the rest of his family, who also lived in the yard, along with my cousin and her boyfriend. There were two houses in the yard: my cousin and her boyfriend lived in a one-bedroom house, while the rest of the man's family occupied the larger house.

During this time, my cousin's boyfriend's sister and I shared a room while my cousin was in the hospital. I had always been an early sleeper. One night, I went to bed, leaving my cousin's boyfriend's sister sitting outside with her family. While I was sleeping, I felt someone pulling my panties down. I grabbed the person's rough hand and began to cry saying *"No, stop what you are doing"*. The man whispered that he would not hurt me. When I tried to yell, he covered my mouth with his hand as he raped me. As I fought back, he pinned me down to the bed with his weight. I started crying and continued to say no as he raped me. The experience was so painful. I thought he was going to suffocate me to death if I did not let him do as he willed. At that moment, I felt helpless as there was no one there to fight for me. It felt surreal, like a nightmare. I later discovered that it was my cousin's boyfriend's cousin, Parlin Daisee, who had forcefully taken my virginity that night. I moaned and groaned from the pain he inflicted. The next morning, I woke up feeling sore and sad, but I didn't tell anyone what had happened out of shame and embarrassment. I remained quiet and withdrawn all day, and everyone assumed that I was upset because my cousin was in the hospital. The man who committed the rape acted as if he had no idea what was troubling me. Unfortunately, this traumatic experience did not end there.

The following night, my cousin's boyfriend, Saye James Mehn, also came into the room and raped me. These two men showed no remorse. I became their object of abuse for two consecutive nights. To this day, I still struggle to understand how and why this happened to me. It felt like a setup, especially since my cousin's boyfriend's sister was supposed to be sleeping in the room with me. I have never spoken to anyone about this incident until the writing of this book. After my cousin was discharged from the hospital, I did not tell her what had happened while she was away. I spent some time with her before receiving a message from my mother, indicating that my foster mother wanted me to return to Monrovia. I left Ganta and went back to Gipo before being sent to my foster mother in Monrovia. My return to Barnesville was filled with excitement, as I was warmly welcomed by my foster family, the church, and the neighbors. However, the experience in Ganta, Nimba County, would forever leave a scar on my mind.

Although I returned to my foster family and was excited to be home again, I was no longer the same person. I felt a deep sense of shame and guilt that weighed heavily on me. The sexual assault I endured at the hands of those two men stripped away my self-worth. I found myself pretending to have a childhood boyfriend or a first love, much like Gama and Faith, but it was all an act. I was merely trying to appear normal, like everyone else. This trauma lingered with me for many years, extending into my adulthood. I never confided in anyone about my pain. It took me years after the incident before I could engage in any sexual relationship with a man. People often labeled me as secretive, assuming I had a hidden romantic partner since no one knew about my boyfriend. However, that was far from the truth; I was shattered inside from the molestation and lacked the courage to share the burdens I carried. At that time in the Liberian society, when someone is sexually molested and speaks out, they often become the target of blame, facing ostracism instead of support. Keeping this information to myself and my inability to speak out eroded my self-confidence. It is crucial to talk to the right people when faced with such traumatic experiences.

My lack of self-confidence, stemming from the trauma of being raped by two men, was one of the weapons my husband wielded against me throughout our marriage and during our divorce. Before we separated, I was genuinely happy with the man I married, appreciating his outspoken nature. I viewed him as my voice, the one who would present me positively to the world. As a devoted wife, I supported him from behind the scenes, loving and respecting him to the point where I rarely made decisions without informing him first. Unfortunately, he never reciprocated the love and care I offered for so many years. He often spoke poorly of me and treated me as if I were worthless. The most painful part was that I accepted his behavior, fearing that he would leave my life. I frequently told my children and friends that I did not want a divorce, primarily because I was afraid of losing the man I considered my voice. Once he realized my desire to keep our family intact, he exploited it, disparaging me both in private and in front of our children on a daily basis. He was adept at knowing when and where to speak. His treatment of me in public or at church was markedly different from how he behaved at home or in front of his friends and our children—he was a master of pretense. On one occasion, he disrespectfully called me an idiot in front of his sister-in-law, who was visiting from Liberia. That insult was deeply humiliating, and I felt embarrassed in front of our guest. I chose not to confront him until we returned home that evening. This incident occurred after I had taken his sister-in-law to visit him at his office. Before we left, she jokingly asked, *'Aren't you going to kiss our husband goodbye?'* To which he replied, *'Don't you know that I married an idiot?'*

When he returned home that evening, I confronted him about the statement he made in front of his sister-in-law. His response was, *"What do you expect when you don't behave right?"* I was left confused by his implication that I was not behaving appropriately. Kissing him in his office or on the street was never part of our routine. This incident was just one of many instances of disrespect I endured during my marriage to Reverend Samuel Siebo. I never received a genuine apology from my husband for his disrespectful behavior towards me; all I encountered was manipulation.

Writing about my experience of sexual assault and the abuse I endured in my marriage is incredibly challenging for me. However, I recognize that these past experiences are tools the devil uses to torment my self-worth. By sharing my story, I expose his schemes, break the chains of bondage, and free myself from his hold. I refuse to return to Egypt and become a slave to the Pharaoh of my past. I must move forward because dwelling on my past is akin to slavery. I also understand that there are women out there who may be facing similar circumstances and need to hear this message. I want you to know that you are not to blame for what happened to you in your childhood or in past relationships. Until you realize that it is not your fault, you will continue to hinder yourself from reaching your true potential and the many glorious opportunities that God has in store for you. The enemy (the Devil) wants you to blame yourself by clinging to your past, causing you to miss the blessings that lie ahead. I want to share a powerful insight from my pastor, Bishop Chris Daigle: *"The devil doesn't care about your past; although he reminds you of it, he is more interested in your potential and your future."* The devil uses reminders of your past as a distraction from your potential. Do not let him prevent you from moving forward, which is essential for your growth.

I am uncertain whether my traditional upbringing influenced the events that transpired in Ganta or elsewhere. Even as a Christian, I failed to grasp the severe repercussions of my idolatrous foundation until I encountered difficulties in my marriage, which I will elaborate on in upcoming chapters. The more I immersed myself in spiritual matters, the more apprehensive I became, particularly when I reflected on the idolatry I was subconsciously involved in while in Gipo. Growing up in a polygamous household, steeped in idol worship, felt like a double-edged curse. It is well-known that our past can haunt us—whether it be personal, parental, or generational. A person's history can catch up with them when they least expect it. As children of God, if we do not confront our past appropriately by grounding ourselves in the Word of God, it can cause us harm. The only weapon we need to combat the enemy is the Word of God. As I delved into the implications of generational curses, I became acutely aware that two of my older sisters had experienced divorce, and the third was on the brink of it. This realization instilled in me a profound fear of divorce. I wanted to avoid the topic entirely; I would rather endure any hardship than face divorce. I began to combat my fear with fear itself to stave off divorce. In my mind, I pondered what others would say if my husband divorced me, and my internal response was a resolute, "No, I cannot divorce." These thoughts consumed me. I resolved to do anything to ensure my husband's happiness, even if it meant sacrificing my own. I mistakenly believed that fighting my fear with fear was the best approach. It is no wonder that Dr. D.K. Olukoya describes fear as faith in failure. My fear truly manifested as faith in failure, for the more I endeavored to please my husband by diminishing my own needs, the worse my situation became. It seemed that my kindness only diminished his regard for my humanity. Pastor Joel Osteen wisely states, *"Anything you feel you must have to be happy can be used against you by the enemy."* Samuel became increasingly insensitive in his words, both to me and about me, in front of our children, family, and friends. As believers in Christ Jesus, when we attempt to control what is beyond our grasp and exclude God from the equation, we inadvertently grant the enemy a foothold over us, leading to merciless consequences due to our ignorance. The good news is that we serve a trustworthy God. He is willing to transform our circumstances for our benefit when we recognize our need for Him and commit ourselves to His guidance.

PART II
LIFE UPENDED

CHAPTER 3

BARNESVILLE MY NEW HOME

After more than three years of gradual assimilation, I had finally settled into my new life as a member of the house and the community in Barnesville. I reassured myself that there was no turning back to my former life in Gipo. Gipo was increasingly becoming a mere figment of my imagination, even though my mother still resided there. I often found myself haunted by recurring dreams of Gipo, my friends, and the enigmatic river that was said to harbor people within its depths. The memories of being violated by my cousin's boyfriend and his cousin continued to plague me. The more I attempted to forget, the more those thoughts persisted. Yet, I knew I had to discover a way to move forward without being hindered by what I still referred to as a nightmare. As my life began to regain its balance, I was astonished by how swiftly the years seemed to pass, particularly following my father's death just a few months after my arrival in Monrovia.

At Barnesville Public School, I gained recognition for my performances in various programs and events. Although I didn't participate in sports like many of my classmates, I consistently took part in the school's activities, including Flag Day, Unification Day, Gala Day, and the school closing ceremony. I was well-liked by my peers, and I held a strong sense of self-love. Academically and socially, I was thriving. During school programs, I often graced the stage three to four times, whether singing in the choir, performing solo, or acting in dramas alongside classmates such as Emanuel Gray, Peter Logan, and Leon Judodoe. In many of these performances, I frequently took on the role of the main character. Teacher Washington, with whom I had a past incident, became my biggest supporter due to my outstanding performances. He even encouraged other students to emulate my example, likely forgetting our earlier encounter. I genuinely enjoyed my time at school and was fully engaged in its activities. I formed numerous friendships, both with boys and girls, during my elementary years. I was vibrant, cheerful, and open to making new friends. Among my many companions, Venus Louis stood out as my closest friend. We shared recess and walked home together every day. After graduating from Barnesville Public School, I transitioned to the local junior high school in Barnesville Estate.

My journey through junior high began in 1988 at the Edward Jonathan Goodridge Memorial Jr & Senior High School in Barnesville Estate. This period was a transformative experience for me, as my femininity became increasingly noticeable. Boys at school and in the neighborhood began to recognize me not just for my talents or academic achievements, but primarily for my femininity. They would approach me with letters, often filled with romantic verses, attempting to express their feelings. However, after experiencing sexual molestation in Ganta Nimba at the hands of my cousin Oretha Quaye's boyfriend, Saye James Mehn, and his cousin, Parlin Daisee, I became withdrawn. I found it difficult to show any emotion towards boys at school or in the community. The trauma left a deep scar on my psyche; I no longer felt comfortable discussing relationships like my friends or even my sister, who lived with me. Gradually, I lost the motivation to participate in school activities and stopped caring about many aspects of my life. My focus shifted solely to obtaining an education, attending church, and looking out for myself. The experience of sexual molestation transformed me into a different person, hardening me as a young woman to the extent that I began to harbor resentment towards men.

Despite being affected by the sexual assault I endured, I remained determined in my academic pursuits, masking my struggles with a facade of normalcy. In seventh grade, I had a close friend named Weddi, along with a few acquaintances. Weddi lived with her family in our neighborhood, and we often walked to school together, studied side by side, shared meals, and exchanged our dreams. There were times when neither of us had money for lunch, nor could we bring food from home. Like my foster mother, Weddi's family faced financial hardships and fought for survival. Many days, as we walked home from school, we would venture into the bushes to search for palm kernels, which we would break open and eat for lunch or as snacks. Too often, we arrived at school hungry and returned home with empty stomachs. Unfortunately, my friend Weddi did not finish the seventh grade; her family moved away, and I lost touch with her.

After Weddi's departure from Barnesville, I formed

a friendship with Comfort Saye. Our bond developed at the end of seventh grade and continued through eighth grade. Unlike my relationship with Weddi, we didn't spend much time together. Comfort was somewhat more mature and was grappling with various personal issues. In an effort to move past the trauma of the sexual assault incident, I began to emerge from my shell and engage in social events at school and within our church community.

At some point during eighth grade, rumors circulated about armed men, including Liberians, training in Burkina Faso. Soon after, we started hearing reports of rebels invading Liberia, aiming to overthrow a government that had been in power for nearly a decade. At that time, we were unaware of the implications of civil war for our country, so we didn't take the news seriously.

As months passed and reports of the rebel forces advancing toward Monrovia increased, life in the capital began to shut down. When the rebel group was just a few miles from Monrovia, foreign business owners started withdrawing their investments from the country. Consequently, we found ourselves reliant on local businesses, which soon faced shortages of supplies. Many people began heading toward the rebel groups, where they believed they could find food that had been looted from various storage facilities.

Those who feared the Charles Taylor rebel group sought refuge with Prince Johnson's faction in Caldwell. One morning in 1990, amidst the civil war, we awoke to find ourselves surrounded by Charles Taylor's rebels. They had taken over our community and were instructing everyone to go to Fendell Campus, as they were preparing to attack Monrovia via Barnesville.

Heeding the rebels' instructions, we quickly packed a few items from our homes and began our journey toward Mount Barclay via Johnsonville. Upon reaching the main dirt motor road, we encountered a massive crowd traveling from Barnesville and Gardnersville toward Johnsonville. During our long trek to Fendell, Gama and I struggled to keep up with our family, who were far ahead. As we approached the border between Johnsonville and Mount Barclay, we overheard murmurs about a checkpoint where the rebel group was stopping and interrogating people. Those who were unfortunate enough to attract their attention faced summary execution.

At that checkpoint, we arrived at the infamous *'God Bless You Checkpoint or gate'* on the road to Fendell. To our astonishment, we found our entire family and relatives, along with others from the Barnesville Oldfield Community, sitting there while the rebels shouted at them. They accused them, saying, *"You are the ones who enjoyed the government's money; we will deal with you today."* One of the rebels seized my mother's arm, shaking it as he remarked, *"Look at all this juicy flesh."* In that moment, I witnessed the miraculous workings of God, who appeared in a magnificent way.

As we drew closer to the checkpoint, I heard one of

the rebels speaking in Mano, declaring, *"We will not joke with these ones today."* I responded in Mano, asking, *"Why?"* He turned to me, surprised, and said, *"Oh, you speak Mano?"* I affirmed, introducing myself as Yah Legay. He then signaled me to come closer. I replied, *"But you have my people sitting over there on the ground."* He inquired, *"Who are your people?"* I explained, *"All the people sitting down there."* When he asked how I was related to them, I told him that we all lived together as a family. Remarkably, he freed everyone that day, and we continued our journey to Fendell.

On that fateful day, it was undeniably the Lord's doing. The rebels showed no regard for anyone, whether you were Mano, Gio, or belonged to the Bassa tribe; they acted with impunity, committing acts of violence such as killing, raping, and imprisoning those they suspected of being their enemies, government employees, or supporters of the government. Following my harrowing experience at that checkpoint and the subsequent ceasefire, I encountered several individuals who expressed their gratitude for my efforts in saving them that day. Remarkably, these were people I had never met before.

While at Fendell Campus, Gama and I made the decision to travel to Nimba in search of food. After informing our parents, they consented to our journey into the countryside. One evening, Gama and I boarded a large rebel truck bound for Nimba from Fendell. The journey took us a couple of days to reach Gipo, and a week later, we discovered that no vehicles were permitted to enter Monrovia from the territory controlled by Charles Taylor's rebels. We learned that shortly after we departed from Fendell that evening, the Peacekeeping Forces, part of a coalition of West African nations known as the Economic Community of West African States Monitoring Group (ECOMOG), launched an attack on Charles Taylor's rebels in the area, liberating the displaced persons' camp at Fendell.

In the aftermath of the liberation of Fendell and surrounding areas near Monrovia, all vehicles were barred from entering the city from rebel-held territories. Consequently, Gama and I found ourselves trapped behind enemy lines, remaining in Gipo for nearly two years.

During our time in Gipo, we regularly visited the farm with my mother and other relatives. There was little else to occupy our days, so we would spend our afternoons at the farm and return to town in the evenings. To assist with my mother's farming efforts, I joined a group of young people who had returned to the village from Monrovia and other cities to be with their families, displaced by the ongoing civil war. When Gama and I arrived in Gipo, my father's house was filled with my siblings, who had also come back to the village due to the conflict. Although Gama and I had not intended to stay in Gipo for long, the time spent with my siblings was deeply fulfilling. We connected over shared experiences, often sitting under the moonlight, engaging in conversations where everyone shared their stories about the war and their journeys to Gipo. While we did not bathe in the Wehyee River as I had with my friends during my childhood, my siblings and I washed our clothes in the river whenever laundry was needed. I missed hanging out with my friends as we once did. I heard that Yar Martha was living on a farm in the forest with her family because of the war, and Yei Nancy had married and settled in a nearby town. Gama and I did not return to Monrovia until January 1992, when access was granted from Charles Taylor's area. Fortunately, we arrived back in Monrovia just in time for the new school year. Once there, I registered for the 9th grade at my former school, Edward Jonathan Goodridge Memorial Jr & Senior High School in Barnesville Estate.

When I entered the 9th grade, I truly began to flourish. This year was significantly more enjoyable for me, filled with numerous cookout events and other class gatherings. We affectionately referred to our cookout as *'Country Cook,'* where every student contributed to the meal preparation. Some classmates brought rice, canned goods, fish, and even money to help with the costs. The boys in my class were not only friendly but also quite jovial, creating a lively atmosphere. Academically, the class was competitive, and I found myself motivated to keep up with the bright boys around me. This drive pushed me to work harder, and ultimately, I succeeded. On several occasions, Nanaka and Alexander would tell me that I was the only girl in our class to achieve a passing grade on a test.

In the 9th grade, I had the privilege of studying alongside two exceptionally quick-witted classmates, Frances Nanaka and Alexander Weah. Our study sessions often sparked lively debates on various topics, as each of us sought to articulate our points convincingly. Both Nanaka and Alexander lived in the same community as I did, which made it easy for me to turn to them for assistance whenever I struggled to grasp a concept in class. Their support proved invaluable to my academic journey.

I also had a female friend named Victoria Eliot in ninth grade. While Victoria and I spent some time together socially, we did not study together. She lived near the Ben and Stop junction with her family, while I resided in Barnesville Oldfield with my parents.

After completing 9th grade, our lives were disrupted by another outbreak of war in October 1992, involving the rebel forces led by Charles Taylor and the ECOMOG Peacekeeping Forces. This conflict, referred to as Operation Octopus by Taylor, was so severe that we were forced to flee Barnesville and seek refuge in the capital city of Monrovia. In Monrovia, we found shelter with my foster relatives on Randall Street in Central Monrovia. We remained there for several months until a ceasefire agreement was reached between the government and the rebel forces.

 Life in Monrovia during this period was an extraordinary experience for me. We could easily stroll to any store or supermarket for our shopping needs. It was my first encounter with a supermarket, and I vividly recall the moment I saw apples for the first time. The store's interior was stunning; it was cool and filled with a delightful aroma. Although we had left our home in search of refuge in Monrovia, this time became one of the most memorable chapters of my life as a young woman. I had the chance to visit the Ministry of Education Beauty School, where I had my hair washed and styled. During this period, I was introduced to what I considered true civilization. I noticed a bathroom cleaner and a mop in the supermarket, which was a revelation for me. In Barnesville, we did not have an indoor bathroom, so I was unfamiliar with the specialized tools used for cleaning. We would clean our house floors with old towels, using buckets of water and scrubbing on our knees. Despite the challenges posed by the Octopus war, it inadvertently opened my eyes to modern life in the city of Monrovia, where I had lived for nearly ten years.

After several months of profound life experiences in the City of Monrovia, amidst the sounds of gunfire and bombs echoing from the suburbs, we were informed that it was safe to return to Barnesville following yet another ceasefire agreement between the warring factions in the Liberian Civil Wars. Although I was reluctant to leave Monrovia and return to Barnesville, as I had done several years prior, I had no choice but to accompany my foster parents back to our home. Once we settled in, it wasn't long before we had to start preparing for school. Given my experiences living on Randell Street, I was not eager to return to E. Jonathan Goodridge. Instead, I yearned to attend school in Monrovia, like my cousins Hawa Taylor and Lisa Greene, who had relocated from Caldwell to Barnesville due to the war.

Unfortunately, I lacked the financial means to enroll in the school they attended, AME Zion High School on Benson Street, a private Christian institution. My desire to study in the city intensified after the Octopus War, prompting me to discuss my aspirations with everyone I met. *"Why don't you consider William V.S. Tubman High School in Sinkor?"* someone suggested. While I contemplated this option, the distance and daily transportation costs made it unaffordable. Ultimately, I decided to apply to Matilda Newport High School after participating in a school tour.

One might wonder why I chose to leave a school within reach to pursue my education at a high school in the city. Reflecting on my earlier life experiences on Randall Street during the Octopus War, I was determined not to return to Barnesville, let alone complete my high school education at E.J. Goodridge. I envisioned myself as someone who belonged in the city—and I was eager to be there. During my visit to tour Newport High School on Newport Street in downtown Monrovia, I fortuitously met a former schoolmate, Henry Torh, who became a pillar of support throughout my high school journey. Henry was one of the kindest young men I encountered in Liberia. Although he had graduated from Goodridge and was not continuing his education, he was living in Central Monrovia on Water Street, selling used sneakers on Randall Street. He provided me with both recess and transportation to and from Barnesville every day.

My experience at Newport High School was remarkable. Here I was, a girl from Gipo, now attending school in the heart of the city—a dream for many village girls. While I didn't make a large number of friends at Newport, I did form strong bonds with a few exceptional classmates, including a bright student named Samuel Dorbor, along with others whose names have faded with time. At Newport High, we walked everywhere, traversing the city from one end to the other. I often arrived at school early, stopping by Henry's selling spot before making my way up the hill to Newport Street. In fact, I discovered a shortcut between houses that led me directly to Newport Street by the school. Henry frequently walked with me in the afternoons, and by the time school ended, he would be right there, ready to take me to the bus for my journey home. His presence became so prominent that my classmates began to tease me. Whenever they spotted him, they would whisper to one another, *"Look who's standing over there—Jennifer's man, of course."* Then one would quip, *"This guy won't let anyone else talk to her. What kind of man is this?"* And we would all share a laugh. The experience was truly wonderful!

Throughout my academic journey, I have been immensely grateful for the blessings I have received. As I neared the conclusion of my 10th-grade year, a remarkable scholarship opportunity emerged through the African Methodist Episcopal Church (AMEC) Lay Organization for Monrovia College and Industrial Training School. The Lay Organization of the AME Church in Liberia was offering scholarships to high school students within its community. Upon discovering this opportunity, Gama and I decided to apply, and we were fortunate to be accepted after meeting the scholarship requirements and participating in several interviews. However, the final decision hinged on the results of the entrance exam for Monrovia College and Industrial Training School. Once the exam results were announced and I successfully passed, I presented my results to Mrs. Elaine Wilson, the chairperson overseeing the scholarship. That day, I was awarded a full scholarship for 11th grade at Monrovia College, with the potential for extension into 12th grade, contingent upon my academic performance at the end of the 11th-grade school year.

With Gama and I on a full academic scholarship at Monrovia College and Industrial Training School, a religious high school that also offered vocational training, it felt like a dream come true. This was especially significant for me, as I was determined to make my mother proud. Our daily routine began at 4:00 AM, when we would carefully pack our uniforms in plastic bags to keep them dry and clean. We walked from Barnesville Oldfield to Gardnersville and Barnesville Junctions to catch a bus to Monrovia. By the time we arrived, we were often drenched from head to toe due to the heavy torrential rains. We would then visit our cousin Musu Greene, who lived on Clay Street behind the Monrovia College fence, to change into our uniforms. This process became a tiring routine, both physically and mentally. However, when you desire something deeply, you must be willing to sacrifice your comfort and dignity to achieve it.

Unmasking: A Journey Through Fear to Embrace Reality

Traveling from Barnesville to Monrovia proved to be quite costly, and even the bus rides to and from Monrovia were challenging. On several occasions, I had to stay overnight in Monrovia with my sister, Marie Legay, who was living in a one-bedroom apartment in Slipway at the time. My friend Henry also graciously offered me a place to stay during the week, allowing me to return to Barnesville on weekends. I concealed this part of my educational journey from my parents, knowing they would have been upset if they had found out. Our mother would never have approved of me living with a man, so I fabricated a story, telling her that I was staying with my sister for school and returning home on weekends. Aside from the transportation difficulties, the school experience was wonderful. I was almost always the first to arrive in class, as we woke up early each day to ensure we reached Monrovia on time. One morning, only two or three of us were present when a new female classmate walked in. She greeted us and approached me, extending her hand. "Good morning, I'm Wilhelmina Bryant, and today is my first day in this class," she said. She shared that she had just moved from Buchanan to Monrovia. I felt a wave of relief and happiness at the prospect of making a friend, as I had been feeling quite isolated in class.

Monrovia College, commonly referred to as MC, was one of the premier high schools in Liberia. We were fortunate to have exceptional teachers both before and in the years following the Liberian Civil Wars of the 1990s and early 2000s. During my first year, we had two remarkable instructors: Mr. Banks, who taught history, and Dr. Emmanuel Ekyinabah, who taught biology, both in the 11th grade. Their subjects were quite challenging, requiring us to thoroughly understand the material and be able to recite it to succeed in their tests. Often, my classmate Wilhelmina and I studied together, developing a friendly rivalry. If I scored lower than Wilhelmina on a test, I would feel frustrated, and she felt the same way. This competitive spirit motivated us to study harder, both together and individually. We successfully completed 11th grade and continued on to 12th grade together. However, during my senior year, I struggled to maintain my grades, while Wilhelmina encouraged me to improve. Thanks to her support, I was able to turn things around and finish the year successfully.

By the time I began my 11th grade at Monrovia College, my mother and the rest of my foster family were aware that Henry was my boyfriend. They liked him, but they were unaware that I was living with him while attending school in Monrovia. Henry was incredibly supportive of my education, ensuring I had everything I needed for my studies. He bought me every new pair of women's shoes that arrived in Monrovia. I never went hungry during our time together; he always made sure there was cooked food for me, especially on days when he didn't go out to sell. I didn't have to fetch water, as we were concerned someone might see me and inform my mother. At that time, there was no running water in Monrovia, but Henry ensured I had water whenever I needed to bathe, either by purchasing it or fetching it himself. Whenever I was with Henry, I stayed in his room. The house had multiple rooms with various tenants, and I wanted to avoid running into anyone who might report my presence to my mother.

During the second semester of my 12th grade, I noticed a girl from Henry's tribe visiting his selling area in Downtown Monrovia. When I inquired about her, he assured me she wasn't coming to see him. However, later, someone in his apartment mentioned that occasionally, when I went to Barnesville on weekends, a girl would come to him, and they would leave together. One day, while I was in the room, someone from the apartment called for me and intentionally walked toward the living room, a common gathering area for the residents. To my surprise, it was the girl I had seen at Henry's selling place. Henry wasn't there with her, but it became clear she had been visiting him even on days I was present, as I typically stayed in the room at his house. When she noticed me, she quickly got up and left. When Henry returned home, I informed him about the girl's visit, but he claimed he had no idea why she was there. I chose to believe him.

As high school drew to a close, I felt a mix of excitement and anticipation. My grades were strong, and graduation was just around the corner. In early 1996, we took the National Exam, known as the West African Examination Council (WAEC) Exam. Bursting with enthusiasm, I decided to visit my boyfriend, Henry, in Monrovia. After a long bus journey, I finally arrived on Water Street in downtown Monrovia.

Upon entering Henry's apartment building, I noticed the surprised expressions on the faces of the women in the kitchen. I greeted them and headed straight to Henry's room. As I approached, I saw that the door was ajar. Without knocking, I pushed it open, only to find a girl sitting on Henry's bed, peering through the crack of the door. This was the same girl Henry had insisted he was not involved with. Although Henry was not in the room at that moment, the girl quickly exited and slipped into one of the other guys' rooms.

When Henry arrived, he feigned ignorance about the situation. Anger surged within me, and I didn't allow him to explain. I pushed him onto the bed and began to hit him, unleashing a torrent of insults. Afterward, I grabbed my bag and returned home to Barnesville, choosing not to share what had transpired with anyone. I resolved to cut ties with him.

A few days later, Henry came to my family's yard, asking me to visit him so we could talk, but I firmly refused. Realizing I was serious about my decision, he approached my mother a week later, explaining the situation and offering his apology. After a conversation with my mother, I decided to accept his apology, as I had genuine feelings for him; he was caring and attentive to my well-being. However, my trust in him had been shattered.

Before the incident, I had believed he was the man I would spend my life with—my first true love.

Unmasking: A Journey Through Fear to Embrace Reality

Despite everything, we continued our relationship. Once I finished school, I moved back to Barnesville and found myself visiting Monrovia less frequently.

As I awaited graduation day, another war erupted. This conflict began on the morning of April 6, 1996, and it was during this tumultuous time that I lost contact with Henry. Life became increasingly challenging in Monrovia. One day, I decided to venture to Paynesville Red Light to look for people from Gipo, who frequently came to Monrovia to sell their goods. Fortunately, on that day, I encountered my cousin Alfred Zankpah's girlfriend, who had traveled from Gipo to sell her wares. Although I didn't know her personally, the locals from Gipo informed me of her identity. We quickly formed a connection. She encouraged me to gather my belongings, offering to cover my transportation costs to Gipo. I informed my foster mother of my plans to go to Gipo, and we departed the following day. I spent a month in Gipo, during which I discovered that Henry was staying at the girlfriend's family home in Gardnersville. After confirming this information, I wrote him a letter, expressing my decision to end our relationship. I entrusted the letter to my cousin Alfred for delivery. Thus, this marked the conclusion of my relationship with Henry.

During my time in Gipo, I made several trips to Monrovia to sell goods I had gathered from the farm. On one of these trips, I encountered some of my classmates at the Red Light, who informed me about our new graduation date. I returned to Gipo and stayed there until just a few days before graduation, when I came back to Monrovia. After graduation, I made a couple more trips to Gipo before finally returning to Monrovia to either start college or seek employment after high school.

One day, while visiting family members in the Red Light area, I ran into a girl I knew from Goodridge during my junior high school years. She invited me to walk with her to one of her friend's business centers, and I agreed. The establishment sold alcohol, barbecue beef, chicken, fish, and pork. Once inside, we sat down and began chatting. The business owner was warm and welcoming.

As we enjoyed our conversation, two gentlemen entered the place, took their seats, and placed their orders. After a few minutes, they called the owner over to ask if we would like to join them at their table. When she returned to us, she mentioned that one of the men had inquired about me and expressed a desire to speak with me. I chose to ignore his invitation. Realizing I wasn't interested in joining them, he approached our table instead.

"Hello, beautiful ladies," he greeted us, shaking our hands and engaging us in conversation. When the other ladies noticed his intention to have a more intimate discussion with me, they discreetly left the table to give us some privacy.

He introduced himself to me, and we exchanged information. A week later, while sitting at home, a sleek SUV drove into our yard in Barnesville, capturing everyone's attention. No one knew who the driver was, and I was equally in the dark. I had no idea what vehicle the mysterious man I met at the business center a week prior was driving. As he parked and stepped out of the SUV, my eyes widened in surprise! He approached me with confidence, a broad smile plastered across his face. I thought to myself, *'Not in front of my parents.'* I felt embarrassed, thinking that he would want to be romantic in front my parent. He greeted everyone in the yard and chatted with me briefly before leaving. I noticed he had a few people in the car that day.

It seemed he wanted to demonstrate that he was serious about what he had said to me at the business center. Thus began my relationship with the senator, which continued until Samuel Siebo entered the picture.

CHAPTER 4

How I Met My Husband

Life often presents us with unexpected challenges, particularly in the realm of romantic relationships. After experiencing heartbreak and an unsuccessful courtship with Henry, I felt as though God had intervened to heal my wounded heart. It was early 1998, and I was sitting in the office of the executive director of the National Investment Commission of Liberia, where I worked as a clerk. Suddenly, a coworker entered and said, *"There's someone here looking for you."* Curious, I stood up and stepped outside my office, only to be greeted by my former 12th-grade classmate, Samuel Siebo, who wore a broad smile. Overwhelmed with excitement at seeing him, I exclaimed, *"Oh Siebo! What brings you here?"* He responded, *"I came to look for you."* Initially, I thought he was joking, as we had never shared a close connection during our school days. I assumed he was merely visiting for business and wanted to say hello. Given that our office catered to investors and small businesses, it was plausible he was there for some professional reason. However, he insisted that his visit was solely to see me and that he wanted to talk. His earnest demeanor made it clear he was serious. Intrigued by his passion, I asked, *"Alright, what do you want to discuss?"* He suggested, *"Let's head to the restaurant so we can sit down and talk."* Not wanting to dismiss him, I agreed to accompany him, especially since it was nearly time for my lunch break. I quickly returned to my office to inform my boss that I was stepping out for lunch.

Back in the lobby, Samuel stood waiting for me, a broad smile still plastered across his face. Beside the office building was a private restaurant. Not wanting to stray too far from work, we walked to the restaurant and found a table. Out of the corner of my eye, I noticed Samuel glancing at me as if he had never seen me before. After we were seated, the waitress approached us with a warm greeting and asked, *"Hello, can I get you a menu?"* Samuel replied, *"Not right now, we'll let you know."* I then inquired why he had brought me there on my lunch break if he wasn't planning to eat. He explained that he wanted to discuss something very important. *"Okay, go ahead and tell me what's on your mind,"* I said. *"Are you currently in a serious relationship?"* he asked. I smiled and responded, *"Why are you asking me about my relationship?"* Looking directly into my eyes, he declared, *"I want to marry you."* I laughed and replied, "Marry me? What are you talking about? Is this a joke? Because all the men around here only mention marriage when they want something more physical." His response surprised me: *"That's not the case with me; I'm very serious. I want you to be my wife, not just a girlfriend."* He continued, *"God told me that you are my wife."*

Reflecting on the encounter brings to mind Steven Furtick's sermon titled *"Bent Knees Break Chains."* In this sermon, he discussed the message Joseph's brothers sent him, driven by their fear of his retaliation for the wrongs they had committed against him after their father's death. He remarked, *"When others tell you what God says to them about you as a form of manipulation,"* which perfectly encapsulated my experience. Samuel continued to express how God revealed to him in a dream that I was to be his wife. The conversation seemed endless, making it difficult for me to return to work. To bring it to a close, I suggested, *"Alright, if God has indeed told you that I'm your wife, let's pray about it."* He agreed, and we left the restaurant without him offering me a soft drink. For me, that marked the conclusion of the discussion. However, for Samuel, he had a plan and had identified the person he believed would help him achieve it. He was determined not to relent until he reached his goal.

Weeks passed without any sight of Samuel. One day, while attending a church member's wedding reception on a Sunday evening in April 1998, I noticed a hostess approaching me with a well-dressed man in a suit. To my surprise, it was Samuel Siebo. He was offered a seat at my table, and I initially assumed he was just another wedding guest. However, I soon learned that he had followed me after visiting my house, where he was informed of my whereabouts. My grandmother had sent him with someone to guide him to the reception that Sunday.

"I just wanted to see you so we can continue our conversation from last time," he said.

"Okay," I replied, though I couldn't help but wonder if he was genuinely serious about his talk of marriage. Regardless, I treated him with courtesy

and respect, concealing my lack of interest in both him and his marriage discussions. In the back of my mind, I viewed him like many other men—most seemed primarily interested in pursuing sexual relationships with new women they encountered.

We lingered at the reception for a while before making our way to my home, which was about an hour's walk away. This provided us with ample opportunity to converse as we walked.

He began recounting his story once more, expressing his desire for me to become his wife and envisioning a brighter future together. He promised to buy me a car someday, complete with a license plate reading '*Yah-1.*' I listened intently, feeling at a loss for words as he spoke. His sweet words flowed for over an hour, captivating me with each line. After our lengthy walk, we finally reached home, where grandma was seated on a bench in front of the house. We greeted her, but Samuel initially neglected to introduce himself, as he was preoccupied with searching for Jennifer. Once he was with her, he turned to grandma and said, '*Sorry, grandma, I am Samuel, Reverend Amos Siebo's son.*' Without hesitation, grandma's face lit up with excitement as she replied, '*Reverend Siebo was our pastor, and I knew your mother, Louise Siebo, as well. She was a beautiful woman. You come from a good family,*' she exclaimed, looking at me with a smile. Samuel, however, chose not to elaborate on his family background, a topic he rarely discussed, especially regarding his father's marital history. This was not a conversation he wished to have, particularly about his mother. Grandma was correct; Mary Louise Siebo was indeed Samuel's father's legal wife, but she was not his biological mother. Samuel was the son of Reverend Amos Siebo and his concubine.

On that early evening, Samuel sat with grandmother, engaging in a heartfelt conversation about his father's experiences as a pastor in the church. He shared with her that he was a student at AME University and proudly mentioned that he was the founder and pastor of Faith AME Church in Logan Town. Samuel's sister, Elaine Wilson, is married to Presiding Elder George Wilson, a beloved figure in the AME Church in Liberia. Both Elaine and George were recognized for their significant leadership roles within the church community. After a meaningful discussion, Samuel expressed his desire to leave, seeking some rest to prepare for the upcoming week's challenges. He and I continued our conversations, often meeting for lunch in Central Monrovia.

Samuel's family connections have earned him the love and respect that would soon play a significant role in the success of his plans. When Samuel departed from my family's home that early evening, my grandmother expressed her excitement and shared her thoughts about the qualities of a good man. Although there was no mention of Samuel's intention to marry me during his conversation with her, she quickly recognized that his visit held deeper significance. She encouraged me to give him a chance at love, believing that if nurtured, something positive could emerge from it. She insisted, 'This is a good boy; he comes from a good family. He may not have much at the moment, but he is in school and has a promising future ahead. It's better to choose someone with whom you can grow, building your life together.' She emphasized that he would be a good match for me because he is a pastor. Her advice was influenced by my relationship with an older man who was a Senator in the Liberian Government, a relationship she doubted would lead to a fruitful future. Deep down within, I felt that he was exploiting me of my youthfulness as many bigshots do to young girls around the world.

What my grandmother didn't understand was that I wasn't seeking a future with this older man. Nevertheless, I appreciated her advice, and it was something I had indeed contemplated: finding a partner with whom I could grow old. At that moment, however, I needed someone who could support themselves and assist me as well. Samuel was not in a position to do that.

Liberia is a challenging place to live, especially in the aftermath of the civil war. Although I had a job with the Liberian government, the pay was often delayed. Civil Service employees sometimes went without their salaries for up to seven months. By the time the paycheck finally arrived, it had already been consumed by what are known as payday loans, leaving me in dire need of assistance to sustain myself.

This older man had already covered a year's worth of tuition and fees for me at the African Methodist

Episcopal Church University and had been helping to meet my daily needs and other essentials. I was not prepared to take on someone who couldn't even manage their own basic expenses. Samuel, a young pastor at a newly established church, was earning less than a thousand Liberian dollars a month—equivalent to about $50 US dollars. Given the hardships in Liberia, he was unable to support himself. All he had to offer were words—words of hope and the promise of a better future, which I believed was indeed possible.

The news about the promising young man, Reverend Amos Siebo, who is the brother-in-law of Presiding Elder George Wilson, quickly spread throughout the family. Almost everyone believed he was the one destined for Yah. As the saying goes, *'the voice of the people is the voice of God'*. I decided to give Samuel the chance to visit so we could get to know each other better. We agreed that he would come over on Sunday afternoons after our church services, and he kept to this commitment religiously. Each Sunday evening, we would sit and talk.

Although I welcomed Samuel into my home on those evenings, I was not ready to abandon my relationship with the older man, nor was I prepared to become intimate with Samuel. However, as Proverbs 16:9 states, "We can make our plans, but God determines the outcome," so it was with my intention to hold onto my older partner.

One Sunday evening in July 1998, Samuel came to

visit during a violent thunderstorm. The weather had turned ominous, with heavy rain pouring down relentlessly, casting a gloomy shadow over the area. At that time, armed robbery was rampant in Monrovia, and people were fearful of walking alone in the dark.

That stormy evening, Samuel and I stayed in the living room until after midnight. Knowing it was impossible for him to return home due to the torrential downpour, I invited him into my bedroom for the night. This decision marked the beginning of our romantic relationship.

When I first met Samuel Siebo, he presented himself well, embodying the qualities every young lady seeks in a partner. What I initially perceived as just another man trying to take advantage of a woman turned out to be the complete opposite.

After several months of courtship and relationship building, Samuel Siebo and I were married on December 19, 1998. Our marriage was youthful and filled with hope. I made a vow to myself and to God that I would never seek divorce, based on the teachings I received in church school and sermons from various pastors, emphasizing that God despises divorce. I prayed sincerely for this commitment and upheld my marriage until unforeseen circumstances arose that were beyond my control. I envisioned a future where I would grow old with my husband, a man who would love me for who I am. However, God guides our paths according to His divine plan and purpose for our lives. Even when we stray from

His intended course, He still connects us in ways that align with His greater design. Nothing occurs outside of God's will. His plan is always the best, even if it may not appear so as it unfolds.

CHAPTER 5

The Fear of Reality

I would like to take a moment to digress, as the truth can often be unpleasant. Before Samuel Siebo approached me with his romantic verses about love and marriage, we were not close friends; we merely met in our senior class. I affectionately refer to him as Siebo, but to me, he was just an ordinary classmate. We graduated from Monrovia College and Industrial Training School in October 1996. Our graduation was delayed, initially scheduled for earlier that year or even in the 90s, due to the intermittent civil wars that plagued Liberia at the time. Although we shared the same 12th-grade classroom, our relationship was limited to that of classmates and fellow members of the AME Church. We took some graduation photos together on that significant day, but unfortunately, those pictures were destroyed during the war. The civil conflict forced schools across the country to shut down for an extended period, which meant we were essentially adults navigating high school.

Samuel was quite talkative in class, loud, and always eager to be noticed. He would often stand at the front of the class to share his thoughts, regardless of their relevance. A highly motivated individual and a goal-oriented person, he carried himself with an air of confidence, especially as a young pastor in the AME Church, which was fitting given that our school was affiliated with the church. I knew this much about him when he first approached me about marriage. However, engaging in a sexual relationship with him without understanding the intricacies of his personal life was one of the most reckless decisions I ever made. After our first romantic encounter, a whirlwind of thoughts flooded my mind. *"Why did I allow myself to be drawn into a relationship with this man who couldn't even afford a can of soft drink on our first lunch date?"* I found myself constantly questioning my choices and worrying about the potential consequences. Samuel Siebo possesses a charming way with words, knowing exactly how to make a woman feel special.

In life, we often make decisions and later reflect on our actions to determine if we made the right choices. When we realize that we may have erred, we sometimes attempt to conceal our mistakes, driven by fear or pride. This was one such instance where I felt I hadn't fully let my guard down. The anxiety of what others might think upon learning that I had engaged in sexual intercourse with a man I barely knew weighed heavily on my mind. The *'what ifs'* began to swirl in my thoughts. I found myself questioning, *"Is he truly sincere about his intentions to marry?"* This was a question that Samuel answered without hesitation. He believed it was time for me to introduce him to my parents, asserting that a single night spent with a woman could be sufficient to build trust and discuss marriage, especially if the man follows his heart.

As I contemplated my next steps, he began to urge me to formally present him to my parents as someone ready to marry me. However, that was one request I was not prepared to fulfill. I was uncertain about my readiness to commit to him as a wife. Several factors weighed on my mind. Firstly, I doubted Samuel Siebo's readiness to settle down as he claimed. Secondly, he lacked the means to support a family. While I was still deliberating, Samuel took it upon himself to write a letter to my parents, introducing himself and expressing his intentions toward me. He delivered the letter by hand and did not inform me until after it had been given to my parents. In any relationship where your opinions are disregarded, it is crucial to pause and establish your boundaries. Address any issues you notice early on in the relationship; if you fail to confront them immediately, they may resurface or escalate into more serious problems that could jeopardize your relationship. Human behavior can become chronic, akin to untreated medical conditions. Behavioral issues in romantic relationships should be addressed and resolved promptly from the outset; otherwise, you risk losing both your marriage and your relationship.

I reflected on my situation, contemplating what would truly be in my best interest moving forward. Should I embrace a struggling young man and embark on a life together, or should I choose to stay with an older man who can provide for me? As I pondered this dilemma, I recalled my grandmother's wise words: *"It's better to choose someone with whom you can grow, building your life together."* While her advice holds merit, its effectiveness hinges on the person you choose to be with. If you find yourself involved with someone who has ulterior motives for being with you, you risk becoming merely a stepping stone for their advancement. When the time comes for both of you to flourish and enjoy the fruits of your labor, they may suddenly deem you unworthy of their company. This was precisely the situation I faced with Reverend Samuel Siebo.

I felt unworthy of my husband the moment he was accepted by the AME Church to run for the position of bishop. He sought a woman connected to influential figures in the church, especially after the 2016 AME General Conference, which catapulted him to fame. His popularity stemmed from the fact that the church had not seen a young man, particularly a US Military Chaplain, vying for the bishopric in a long time, if ever. Samuel decided to pursue the bishopric as an Active-Duty US Army Chaplain of the AME Church upon his return from military deployment in Afghanistan. He was young, energetic, charismatic, and outspoken, which endeared him to the church community. However, this attention inflated his ego—he became self-absorbed and prideful, believing no one in the church was his equal. He felt that everyone envied his newfound status. As his wife, I felt sad for the narcissistic person Samuel Siebo had become.

He expressed to me his need for a woman who would support his ambitions of becoming a bishop. He would say, '*Do you see how many women throw themselves at me at those church conferences? I could easily discard you and marry a bishop's daughter tomorrow. All the unmarried bishops' daughters in the church are looking for a man like me. Keeping you as my wife is a mistake. I need a woman who will accelerate my path to becoming a bishop. I'm not a small man in the church anymore; just wait and see me marry a bishop's daughter and ascend to the bishopric.'*

No matter emotional abuse, I never faltered. I stayed with my husband and attended to all his needs like a good churchgoing wife. Samuel ran for bishop for the first time during the 2016 General Conference of the AME Church. Although he lost that election, he felt a sense of accomplishment as he gained recognition within the church. He believed that all the *'high-class women'* in the AME Church were enamored with him and that even the bishops respected him, considering him their equal.

We inhabit a world rife with cruelty, wickedness, and deceitful individuals. At times, we find ourselves unwittingly allied with our enemies. Family, friends, and those we hold dear can turn against us in an instant, transforming into the very threats we never anticipated. As a newlywed couple, we shared simple meals of dry rice (boiled rice with palm oil) and went to bed after consuming boiled cassava with palm oil when we could not afford a full meal. Whenever our finances allowed, we purchased fish from vendors along the Waterside Bridge in downtown Monrovia—fish that thrived on human waste. This was our only option, as we could not afford the fish from cold storage or marketplaces. During those early days of marriage, we often slept on the floor, yet we found happiness in our shared struggles. We spent hours on the phone, separated by distance but united in our dreams. I devoted myself to fasting and praying, seeking God's blessings for my family and asking Him to elevate my husband in his ministry. Little did I realize that the allure of worldly splendor and the blessings associated with marriage could ultimately lead to its demise. We believers often seek God's guidance for the unknown.

I was unaware of Samuel's ulterior motive for marrying me. Those who seek to connect with you for selfish reasons often perceive in you the wealth and qualities that you may not recognize in yourself. As Bishop TD Jakes wisely stated, *"You see yourself as a person, but many people see you as an opportunity."* Many individuals view you as a pathway to their success, whether through your education, family background, or connections—elements they believe can elevate their lives.

(Throughout my childhood and up until my marriage to Samuel, I lived with a family that owned numerous properties in Liberia. One of the prominent AME Churches in Liberia bears their family name. Additionally, many of their relatives relocated to the United States after the initial war in Liberia. I suspect Samuel was aware of these circumstances, viewing them as his ticket to his dream of coming to the United States. I believe this was a significant factor in his decision to marry me.)

As he began to ascend the career ladder, he started pressuring me to distance myself from my biological mother and siblings, labeling them as a *"poor family."* He often remarked, *"Your family is poor. This is not the family I envisioned when I decided to marry you; I only knew the Greene family. Had I known about your impoverished background, I wouldn't have married you."* I was perplexed by his comments, especially since my foster mother had informed him that she could not make any decisions regarding my marriage without my family's presence. However, Samuel seemed blind to my *"poor"* family, fixated instead on the perceived wealth and opportunities that he believed would propel him to his next level.

My family background was never a secret to Samuel. Anyone who knows me well understands my deep love for my family, especially my mother. Although my parents did not have the opportunity to attend school, I have always cherished and appreciated them for bringing me into this world. I can never conceal my identity or my origins from anyone; I take pride in my roots. Samuel was well aware of my family's history, having met my mother and my oldest brother, who served as the patriarch of our family. My brother candidly expressed that he believed Samuel's proposal to marry me was insincere. He suspected that Samuel was motivated by a desire for promotion within his church or perhaps seeking a visa to travel to the United States. During that time in Liberia, marrying for the purpose of obtaining a US Visitor Visa was quite common, as family and marriage ties to one's home country were significant factors in securing such visas.

In the early to mid-1990s, many young people in Liberia were marrying to facilitate their travel to the US. My brother was convinced that this was Samuel's intention, which led him to withhold his consent for the marriage proposal. I felt a deep disappointment when my brother refused to support my decision to marry. However, with the backing of my mother and a few other family members, I chose to proceed with the wedding. Little did I realize that my brother was perceiving things from a perspective I had not considered. His concerns ultimately proved to be valid. Samuel married me as a means to escape Liberia and seek a new life in the United States, a dream shared by many young Liberians during the war years. It is disheartening to think that someone would use another person as a stepping stone for personal gain, especially when that person is a child of God. God does not overlook the tears of His children.

We got married in December 1998 and January 1999, he was already expressing a desire to travel to the US. Given the hardships in Liberia at that time, I wholeheartedly supported his ambition, as I longed for a better future for our family. Consequently, I collaborated with him to secure a U.S. Visitor Visa. Unfortunately, he was denied a visa in 1999. However, we remained undeterred in our efforts. Together, we fasted and prayed consistently, seeking God's favor for Samuel to obtain a visa. The power of prayer in agreement is profound in any situation. After we prayed together, my husband Samuel found favor with a counselor, and he ultimately received his visa to travel to the US.

CHAPTER 6

A Marriage Filled with Disrespect and Trouble

Disrespect in a marriage can manifest in various ways, often beginning subtly and gradually. It may start with minor misunderstandings or slights that go unaddressed, escalating over time. Reflecting on our relationship, I identified several common symptoms of disrespect:

1. Communication Breakdown: When partners cease to communicate effectively, misunderstandings can foster feelings of disrespect. This includes not listening, interrupting, or dismissing each other's opinions.

2. Unresolved Conflicts: Allowing conflicts to remain unresolved can breed resentment, which may express itself as disrespectful behavior if not addressed constructively.

3. Dishonesty: Lying or concealing the truth can undermine trust, a fundamental element of respect in any relationship. When trust is compromised, disrespect often follows.

4. Selfishness: Consistently prioritizing one's own needs over those of a partner can lead to feelings of being undervalued or disrespected.

5. Lack of Appreciation: Failing to recognize

and appreciate each other's contributions can make a partner feel taken for granted.

6. Infidelity: An affair represents a significant breach of trust and respect, often resulting in the dissolution of a marriage.

7. Control Issues: Attempting to control or manipulate a partner can be a form of disrespect, undermining their autonomy and value as an equal partner.

As a married couple, it is crucial to address these issues early and seek professional help if necessary to prevent the erosion of respect and the potential breakdown of the marriage. Open, honest communication and a commitment to understanding and meeting each other's needs can help maintain respect and strengthen the relationship.

In my own experience, I realized that many of these signs were present in my marriage. I overlooked them, hoping that Samuel would change for the better, but I was mistaken.

The disrespect I endured throughout my marriage to Samuel Siebo did not arise suddenly; it began long before I accepted his marriage proposal. Regrettably, I failed to establish my boundaries, which allowed the situation to deteriorate progressively over the course of our relationship. I overlooked many early warning signs of a toxic partnership. One significant red flag was his decision to reach out to my parents without my consent. Although

Unmasking: A Journey Through Fear to Embrace Reality

I felt uneasy knowing that Samuel had written a letter to them without my approval, I chose to remain silent, hoping he would respect my wishes in the future. In hindsight, that was the moment I should have firmly asserted myself and said, 'No.' My principle was clear: he had no right to share information regarding my personal decisions with anyone without my consent. To my parents, this behavior may have seemed honorable for a young man, as he claimed he wanted to introduce himself to them because he intended to marry me. He stated that he did not wish to hide from anyone. Reflecting on it now, I realize this was merely one of Samuel's manipulative tactics, a facade he maintained in front of family and friends throughout our marriage. He portrayed himself as the sole virtuous individual in our relationship. Even when I was the one working while he stayed home to cook, he insisted he was the only provider for our household. Conversely, if I were at home cooking while he worked, he would still claim he was doing everything for the family. I juggled three jobs to support our home and fund his expensive clothing and suits for outings with his friends. Regardless of my efforts, Samuel never acknowledged my contributions; it was always about him and his inflated sense of self-importance. He was acutely aware of his audience and knew precisely what to say about me to others. Some people believed he did not love me based on his comments, while others thought I had the best husband in the world. He was fully aware of his manipulative behavior.

Whenever he stood before the pulpit to preach, he

was acutely aware of how to present himself as a decent family man. This persona did not develop overnight; it was a behavior he meticulously crafted from childhood. His letter had incited considerable anger from my parents, who were upset with me for refusing to introduce him to them. They perceived my actions as disrespectful. Consequently, they summoned me for a meeting to express their disappointment regarding my reluctance to present this respectful young man to them. This belief is quite common among parents in Liberia: if a man introduces himself to your parents, they assume he is responsible and respectful. I explained my reasons for not formalizing my relationship with Samuel, but my parents felt my justifications were insufficient to deter me from showcasing a man who was already a frequent visitor in my life. I understood their perspective and offered my apology. They accepted it, yet the pressure for me to settle down with this young man intensified. It was no longer just my grandmother urging me; my foster mother, father, and even the young ladies around my age in the family joined in. I recall one of the girls saying, '*If I were you, I would go ahead and get married. The boy is a pastor and comes from a good family. Why wouldn't you want to marry him? Would you prefer to remain involved with that old senator who doesn't seem serious? Can't you see he's living with a woman he isn't married to while keeping you as another girlfriend? Who knows how many other women he's involved with?*'

At that time, Samuel was actively persuading my friends and family to speak to me, as he often did to enhance his image in front of others. They began to express that this might be my only opportunity to get married, warning that if I declined, I might never marry again. It wasn't that I disliked Samuel; rather, I questioned whether marrying him was the right choice for me. This uncertainty lingered in my mind.

Amidst the discussions about marriage, Samuel chose to disregard our initial plans for visitation on Sunday evening, opting instead to visit on random days throughout the week. One Tuesday evening, while he was at my house, we were sitting on the front porch when we spotted the senator approaching from a distance. Uncharacteristically, he wasn't using his vehicle that day. I urged Samuel to leave, but he refused, insisting that I stay put until the senator arrived and tell him to leave because Samuel was present.

As the senator drew closer and Samuel remained, I felt compelled to escape into one of my sister's bedroom. She was one of the young women living in the house. She came outside and informed the senator that I wasn't home. It was clear that the senator had seen me, as he was not far from the house. This incident likely led him to believe I was involved in another relationship, prompting him to keep his distance, which was exactly what my parents desired. With the senator now out of my life, Samuel felt he had complete control over me.

At the time of my sexual involvement with Samuel, I was transitioning between contraceptives, which may have created a gap that resulted in an unplanned pregnancy. By early August 1998, I discovered that I was pregnant. This unexpected development, combined with the advice I received, propelled the decision to marry. We quickly set a wedding date and began planning the ceremony.

One of the advantages of having a wedding in Liberia during that time was the lack of financial burden associated with planning it. Friends and family members whom you invited to be patrons, sponsors, and organizers generously contributed resources for your special day. If you were fortunate enough to have generous supporters, you could even enjoy a celebrity-style wedding. However, it is crucial to consider the life that follows such an impromptu wedding. The very issues you might overlook today could resurface in your marriage, potentially haunting you in the future. While everyone may rally to celebrate your union, it is ultimately you who must navigate the realities of married life.

Reflecting on my own tumultuous marriage, I often pose the following questions to couples preparing for marriage: *"Are you ready to accept your partner as they are, even years down the line? Do you love them for their true self? Is your partner genuinely in love with you, or do they have hidden motives for wanting to marry? Are you prepared to endure dishonesty, infidelity, arrogance, disrespect, and manipulation?"* If you cannot confidently answer 'YES' to these questions, you may want to reconsider your path to a successful marriage.

Unmasking: A Journey Through Fear to Embrace Reality

These were the very questions I failed to address before marrying Reverence Samuel Siebo. I recall a conversation with the late Presiding Elder Topoe Johnson of the AME Church, who also served as Dean of the Bryant Seminary in Liberia. He asked me, *"I heard you are getting married to Siebo. Are you sure you want to marry him? I've noticed that you don't talk much."* I smiled but did not respond to his inquiry, nor did I ask him why he posed such questions. He concluded with, *"I wish you good luck."*

During the October 1992 war in Monrovia, known as Operation Octopus, we fled from Barnesville to central Monrovia in search of safety, as previously mentioned. We remained there until the ECOMOG Peacekeepers and the local community intervened to halt the fighting. Eventually, Barnesville was declared safe for residents to return home. Upon our return, we discovered that my family home had been reduced to ashes, destroyed during the crossfire between the peacekeepers and rebel forces, leaving us homeless. Fortunately, our neighbors generously offered us rooms in their homes within the community. Consequently, we found ourselves sleeping in different houses at night, yet we gathered in our charred yard during the day to cook and carry out our daily activities as best as we could. Each evening, we would retreat to our respective rooms to sleep. A few months later, my mother managed to construct a two-bedroom house in the remains of our yard, where she, her husband, and my grandmother resided, while the rest of us continued to occupy the rooms provided by our neighbors. All my wedding meetings took place in my family's yard.

In the week leading up to our wedding, I received shocking news: Samuel had a daughter he had never mentioned to me. After our last wedding meeting on a Sunday evening, Samuel and his best man, Arthur Butler—who was like a brother to him—walked with me from the meeting place to my home. As I climbed the stairs to enter the house, I overheard Arthur asking Samuel, *"Have you told Jennifer about the little girl?"* It seemed Samuel was reluctant to respond. Arthur continued, *"You know that could cause serious problems in your marriage down the line. It's better to tell her now than later."* Intrigued by their conversation, I walked back to them to listen more closely. I then asked, *"What are you guys talking about, groom and best man?"* Samuel replied, *"I was going to talk to you about this."* *"Talk to me about what?"* I pressed. *"This little girl that her mother forced on me, claiming she's my daughter,"* he explained. My immediate reaction was disbelief. *"If you have a child, why are you just now telling me? And what do you mean her mother forced her on you?"* I felt a surge of anger, but Arthur urged me to calm down and suggested we discuss it later. I decided to drop the issue for the moment, and both Samuel and Arthur left for home. As someone who often seeks to please others, I began to worry about how people would react to any decision I might make regarding the wedding. At that moment, I felt trapped. I thought to myself, *"I'm carrying this man's child, and we've already planned a wedding involving family and friends. What can I do now? What would people say if I backed out at this stage?"* Ultimately, my fear of judgment weighed heavily on my mind, making it difficult to consider ending the wedding.

It is sometimes acceptable to pay attention to the opinions of your children, friends, and family members. However, what truly matters is the outcome of your decisions based on what you hear. You have the power to ignore external opinions and steer your life in the direction that feels right for you. People often project their beliefs about what is best for you, overlooking the fact that you are a complete individual with your own feelings and willpower. There are choices that can lead you to peace and happiness. Allowing others' validation or fear of their judgment to dictate your key life decisions can have lasting negative effects. The small issues we tend to overlook can be detrimental to our well-being. If something matters to you now and makes you uncomfortable, address it immediately. Do not postpone it, as the future will bring its own challenges that you will need to confront. The combination of unresolved past issues and current problems in a marriage can escalate into larger conflicts, potentially leading to divorce.

Initially, I believed we could manage the challenges we faced in our relationship. I told myself, *'I'm willing to accept a stepchild, even though I was not pleased with how the information was presented to me. Therefore, I will proceed with the wedding.'* It is crucial to be mindful of what you overlook in the early stages of a relationship. As Maya Angelou wisely stated, *'When people show you who they are, believe them the first time.'* A person who genuinely loves you will be honest and forthcoming, sharing their life story to prevent any negative feelings from arising later when you hear about their past from other sources. Conversely, those with ulterior motives may present themselves in a deceptive manner, manipulating you into believing they are something they are not. Such individuals may resort to lies and elaborate displays to win you over.

Determined not to dwell on the past, we moved beyond the issue of Samuel not disclosing his child at the outset of our relationship. The wedding ceremonies proceeded as planned. Despite facing obstacles, setbacks, and delays—potential signs of divine warning—we celebrated a wonderful wedding event. Once the ceremony concluded, well-wishers departed, leaving us to embark on our married life. However, we found ourselves without a stable income to start a family. Our only asset was an empty three-bedroom house, which Samuel had secured for eight months. This home was rented for us to move into after our wedding. Before the ceremony, Samuel had sold some rubber from his father's farm, using the proceeds to cover the rent for the house. He also purchased a six-chair dining table set and a mattress, which constituted our initial furniture. We moved into the house the night after our wedding, accompanied by five relatives: his father, my mother, my brother, his sister, and my niece. We slept comfortably on the mattress on the floor, while the others used pieces of sponge to rest. On Sunday morning, we enjoyed leftover food from the wedding for lunch. With a few cups of rice and some cash gifts received during the wedding, we managed to prepare meals for the next three days.

On Wednesday, at the midpoint of the week, there was no food in the house. Samuel and I decided to head into town to seek opportunities. It was the Christmas season in Liberia, and many employers, including government offices, were distributing rice as gifts to their employees. That day, we managed to gather a 100-pound bag of rice, and Samuel also received some monetary gifts, ensuring we had enough food to last through the holidays. However, I found myself pondering, what would happen after the holidays? I was about four months pregnant with our daughter, and as I surveyed our situation, it became clear that we were struggling to take care of ourselves. Fear began to creep in, and I questioned, *"Lord, am I destined to be the subject of mockery so early in my marriage? Please help me."* At that time, I was reluctant to have visitors in our home, fearing they would judge our living conditions and spread gossip throughout the community. I did my best to make our home presentable. We had no living room chairs, only a dining room set. I acquired a large flowerpot, placed a Christmas tree in it, and decorated it. This decoration took up considerable space in the living room, making the emptiness less noticeable. I resolved to find happiness in my marriage, regardless of the challenges we faced. We were excited to be living together, even without the luxuries that others enjoyed. We had no bank account, no money saved, and no business ventures. Our jobs barely sustained us, but we held onto the belief that life would improve someday. Once

Jennifer Yah Legay

Samuel and I committed to working together to cultivate happiness in our marriage, things began to turn around for us. Everything we touched started to flourish.

PART III
Listen and Be Strong

CHAPTER 7

WORK WITH YOUR INTUITION, IT'S GOD TALKING TO YOU

When God brings you to a challenge, He will guide you through it. Marriage is a sacred institution, and God stands firm by His word. One of my favorite verses from the book of Proverbs 18:22 states, *"He who finds a wife finds a good thing and obtains favor from the LORD."* This scripture served as my strength throughout our marriage, especially when we allowed God to take the lead. We experienced favor on all sides, transforming what initially felt like a struggle into success in both Liberia and the United States.

After the Christmas and New Year's holiday, during the first week of January 1999, Samuel woke up and surveyed the land around us. He exclaimed, *"We can establish our farm here."* Fortunately, the land belonged to my family, and we both agreed to create a cassava farm along with a sweet potato garden and other vegetables to ensure we had our own produce. Samuel and my younger brother spent about a week clearing the bushes, covering a significant portion of land, which provided ample space for a large cassava farm.

However, after the arduous task of clearing the land, we realized we lacked the cassava sticks needed for planting. Samuel, a man with a determined spirit, set out to find the cassava sticks. He encountered

Unmasking: A Journey Through Fear to Embrace Reality

a Nigerian man who owned a cassava farm and had everything we required for our own farm and garden. By the grace of God, the man generously provided Samuel with some cassava sticks and accompanied him to our home to assess the space we had available for the farm. After inspecting the expansive area, the man agreed to sell us the cassava sticks at a reasonable price. Although we didn't have the money readily available, we placed our trust in God, believing that He would provide the means to acquire the cassava sticks—and indeed, He did.

Relying on God's miraculous provision for our needs often requires a deep trust in His infinite power and love. It involves recognizing that even when resources appear limited, He possesses the capacity to intervene and meet the needs of His faithful children. This divine provision may not always manifest as a dramatic miracle; rather, it can unfold through unexpected opportunities, the kindness of others, or a renewed sense of resourcefulness. It is a surrender of worry and a profound belief that God will guide us through even the most challenging moments.

This was certainly true for us in our journey of faith. Whenever Samuel preached on Sundays at the church and received a small token or financial handout, we would set aside a portion of that money to purchase Cassava Sticks. With the funds in hand, we would make the hour-and-thirty-minute walk to the Nigerian man's farm. The path to the farm lay directly in front of the Barnesville Health Center, where my foster mother worked. Samuel would lead the way, balancing a bundle of Cassava Sticks on his head, while I followed closely behind, holding a machete. We would chat and laugh as we carried our Cassava Sticks, unbothered by the opinions of others.

I felt no embarrassment or shame in this endeavor, as I believed in the saying, *"there is no food for a lazy man."* However, some viewed our situation as disgraceful, believing it inappropriate for a newlywed couple to rely on farming for survival. My mother often recounted how her coworkers would call her over when they spotted us passing by the health center, teasing her with remarks like, *"Come see your daughter and her husband, and look at him carrying cassava sticks on his head."*

In those moments, I witnessed my husband, Samuel Siebo, humbled by our financial circumstances. He set aside his pride and did what was necessary to care for our family, embodying the roles of both a father and a husband with grace during this challenging period of our marriage.

After several weeks, we successfully completed the planting of our cassava, sweet potatoes, and various other vegetables. It felt miraculous as everything flourished and yielded abundantly. While we awaited the maturation of our cassava farm and garden to provide food for us, we struggled financially and lacked the means to feed our household. Yet, the Lord provided us with sustenance every day, and we never went to bed hungry during those challenging times.

Unmasking: A Journey Through Fear to Embrace Reality

Fortunately, my foster mother had family in the United States. Her younger sister frequently sent barrels filled with all kinds of food for their mother, and my foster mother, who was caring for their aging mother in Liberia, oversaw everything sent back home. Whenever we found ourselves without food to cook, Samuel would walk the ten to fifteen minutes to my foster mother's house to inform her of our situation. She would promptly pack a bag with rice, canned fish, oil, and seasoning for him to bring back. This would serve as our meal for the day, and sometimes it would even include supplies for two days, depending on what she had available.

Visiting my foster mother's house became a regular routine for us. If we didn't go there, we would venture into town to seek help from friends and family for our meals. Poverty is a heavy burden, and I despised the feeling of being poor.

Two weeks after planting all the crops in our garden, Samuel went to Paynesville Redlight to seek food from one of his older sisters who sold palm oil in the market. During his visit, the idea of soap making emerged in their conversation. She agreed to provide us with a five-gallon container of red palm oil for our soap production, with the understanding that we would pay her after selling the soap. Upon hearing this news upon his return, I was filled with excitement. It seemed that we would be able to make the soap, sell it, and use the proceeds to buy food, while also saving some money for our baby. At that time, the AME Church was providing their pastors in the 14th Episcopal District of Liberia with a stipend of $20 United States Dollars every three months, as many of them were pastoring churches that could not afford to pay salaries. Samuel received his stipend a week after discussing soap making with his sister. We used about $15 of that money to purchase the materials for the soap, and we obtained the oil from his sister on credit.

In the evenings, we would burn the oil in our backyard to transform its color from red to clear, allowing it to sit overnight. The following day, we would produce the soap and let it rest again overnight before the children took it around to various communities for sale. Although this process was quite time-consuming, we were thrilled to have a way to secure our meals each day without having to wait until late at night. Samuel's sister and my brother, who lived with us at the time, were incredibly cooperative. They would leave early in the morning to sell the soap and return just in time to prepare for school, as they both attended afternoon classes. Eventually, we realized that we were essentially selling to cover the cost of the oil and our daily meals—it was a hand-to-mouth business. Nevertheless, the soap business proved to be a significant blessing, sustaining us until our farm and garden began to yield produce. Remarkably, we managed all of this during my pregnancy.

Jehovah God's faithfulness is a profound source of comfort and strength for us believers. It enables us to trust in His unwavering presence and guidance, even amidst uncertainty and challenges. He consistently fulfills His plans and promises, even when circumstances appear daunting. Our journey of reaping rewards began not just in our garden, but in every endeavor we undertook. Once we fully surrendered ourselves and entrusted our problems to God, positive changes began to unfold. Opportunities emerged where there seemed to be none. Indeed, God is not like people who may deceive or fail to keep their promises. We raised a hen that produced an abundance of eggs and chicks. From that hen, I enjoyed organic eggs throughout the last term of my pregnancy, and we had enough chicken for our Sunday meals. We unexpectedly became small business owners as our farm thrived, allowing us to sell cassava, cassava leaves, cassava sticks, sweet potatoes, sweet potato leaves, and other vegetables. God manifested His presence in our lives when we took our first steps as husband and wife. Although we didn't have much, we possessed what we needed to survive, and we were grateful. We served God with sincerity and prayed in agreement with His word, and He opened every door for us, providing breakthroughs at every turn.

During the process of harvesting from our farm and selling the produce, our daughter Louise was born on May 30, 1999. The delivery took place at a midwife clinic not far from our home. Although the delivery was managed by a midwife, we were unable to pay the full delivery fees. One thing was clear: God showed up and provided for us in every way. While we were contemplating how to gather the funds for the midwife, something miraculous occurred. My older sister Kou Legay arrived unexpectedly with a carload of various food items and a live goat from the village, without any prior notice of her visit or my recent childbirth. She explained that she had come to surprise us with a gift because she was unable to attend our wedding. Her visit was perfectly timed. We suddenly had a surplus of food that we could share with friends and relatives, ensuring we had enough for a while. The goat was intended for us to cook and invite friends and family for a cookout, but since we owed the midwife, we decided to sell the goat and use the proceeds to cover the birthing fees.

After the birth of our daughter, we began to see more light at the end of our challenging journey. Samuel and I both secured teaching positions at two local AME elementary schools in Monrovia, which were conveniently located near each other. However, these jobs did not offer substantial pay, and our salaries were often delayed. Despite the late payments, we felt fortunate, as it was far better than working for the Liberian government at that time. We were thrilled because our combined incomes, along with the small contributions Samuel received from his church, would be sufficient to meet our needs, especially with our rent renewal approaching. For me, I knew that God was performing a miracle in our lives, and we needed to continue praising and serving Him.

As a believer, it often feels like progress is being made in life, and the word of God is being fulfilled. However, it is during these moments that the devil attempts to divert our focus from God's promises. I assure you, if you remain steadfast and trust in the Most High God, you will witness His glory manifesting in your life. This was a pivotal moment for us; we could feel God's presence guiding us. We had established a budget based on our modest income and felt secure and comfortable. Then, unexpectedly, Samuel was removed from his church due to a dispute with the Chairman of the Board of Directors of the AME Church in Liberia, who was also his mentor. This left us relying solely on our teaching salaries, and Samuel's dismissal from the church negatively affected our family finances.

Upon his dismissal, my primary response was to pray for my husband, knowing his passion for preaching. Although Samuel wanted to fight back, we chose to select our battles wisely. The Holy Scripture cautions us against resisting divine will (Acts 9:5). When we position ourselves against God's purpose or align with someone—be it through marriage, generational ties, or parental connections—who resists that purpose, we inevitably face consequences. I felt disheartened upon hearing the news of Samuel's dismissal, yet I did not lose faith in God. I clung to His promise that He would never leave nor forsake me. Samuel shared my belief that God would pave a way even when it seemed impossible. During this challenging period, God indeed provided for us, filling the gaps in our lives.

It is indeed true that success is assured in unity. When our adversary observed that we remained steadfast in our faith and continued to believe in God for a significant breakthrough, he launched another attack. This time, our landlord presented us with an eviction notice after abruptly terminating our rental agreement without cause. We were merely two months away from our lease renewal, yet the landlord decided against renewing the contract, insisting instead that we vacate the premises so that his family could move in. He returned the remaining payment for the two months, but this situation was incredibly stressful. During that period in Liberia, landlords typically required at least six months' rent in advance for a new lease, and we simply did not have the funds to secure a new rental agreement. However, the truth remains: when God brings you to a challenge, He will guide you through it. God is faithful to His promises. Each time the enemy attempted to bring us down, He provided a way to lift us up.

At that point in our lives, we decided not to stress or worry, as God delivered us swiftly from our predicament. Upon receiving the news, a family friend, Ms. Marayah Fyneah, along with her fiancé, Mr. Franklin Holt, generously offered us a bedroom in their home at no cost. The bedroom was spacious enough to be divided into two rooms, which was our intention. When Marayah and Franklin saw the number of family members we had with us, they kindly provided us with an additional bedroom. It is no secret that our God is the God of sudden miracles. We resided in this home with our family friends from November 1999 until December 2000, after Samuel traveled to the United States.

Samuel had always dreamed of traveling to the

Unmasking: A Journey Through Fear to Embrace Reality

United States of America, even before he and I became husband and wife. Despite his strong desire, he lacked the means and resources to make this dream a reality. After our marriage, he resolved to pursue his aspiration of visiting the U.S. Regardless of where you find yourself in life, God has a rescue plan for you. Sometimes, He blesses you in ways that test your trust in Him to fulfill your requests.

After several months of diligently working to obtain a U.S. Visa, Samuel finally succeeded in getting a U.S. Visiting Visa. However, after he obtained his visa, he realized that he didn't have a place to stay in the U.S. We turned to God Almighty in prayer for provision, and He answered our prayers. Although Samuel had family in the United States, they were unwilling to take him in. Initially, he mentioned that one of his cousins was willing to host him, but he did not have her address. Consequently, during his Visa application process, he used my aunt, Benetta Greene's address as his host residence, and since his cousin later refused to take him in, she graciously welcomed him during his early days in the U.S.

Once he received his Visa, the next challenge was securing a plane ticket. Samuel did not have the funds to purchase one. After waiting for two and a half months without assistance from his family who promised to assist him, we decided to explore other options. We returned our wedding ring to the goldsmith from whom we had purchased it, and he provided us with $200. I reached out to my sisters living in the U.S., and they sent me another $200. Additionally, someone loaned Samuel $300, which he promised to repay once he settled in the U.S. The ticket cost $1,300, so we still needed $600 more.

At this point, we were uncertain about what to do next, so we turned to my foster mother for help. She spoke with her nephew-in-law, the late Reverend James Coleman, who was friends with Mrs. Ophelia Hoff Saytumah, an airline agent in Liberia. He managed to secure the ticket for Samuel, allowing him to pay it back later.

As the travel date approached, Samuel needed money to cover some fees at the airport in Liberia, but we found ourselves short on funds once again. I approached one of our church families, and they generously provided me with $125. This is how God provided the resources for Samuel to travel to the U.S. in September of 2000.

After several months of constant communication while I was in Liberia, my husband Samuel managed to send me some money, which I used to build a three-bedroom house for our family. Now that we had our own home, I decided to ask Samuel for permission to bring his daughter, Ernestine, to live with us. I truly wanted Ernestine and Louise to grow up together and bond as siblings. When I discussed my desire to welcome Ernestine into our home, Samuel seemed hesitant. He expressed his concerns that Ernestine's mother might not approve of her staying with me and feared that she could even wish to harm me, as he believes that she comes from a family that practices voodoo and witchcraft. Another reason for wanting to take Ernestine in my home is that Samuel was not willing to support Ernestine while she was with her mother, and since we had resources through his support, I thought it was good for Ernestine to get the benefit. For some reason, he believes that Ernestine's mother would use his money to bewitch him.

Understanding the God I serve, I assured Him, *"We will be okay, and nothing will happen to us."* He consented to allow me to take Ernestine from her mother to care for her as his wife. By the time I was prepared to bring Ernestine home, she was already with Samuel's mother. I then requested her to bring the child to me, and she complied. Ernestine was just five years old when I welcomed her into my home. During our early years, she and Louise shared the same bed with me until we moved to the USA. In our home, we formed one big, happy family. Samuel would frequently call to speak with me and the children, which brought me immense joy. He was also content, knowing that all the children were growing up together in the same household.

CHAPTER 8

LIFE IN THE U.S., JOHNSON CITY, TENNESSEE

Embarking on a new life in the United States can be a dream realized, yet it is often accompanied by numerous challenges. New immigrants frequently contend with language barriers, which complicate everyday tasks such as shopping and navigating public transportation. This struggle can foster feelings of isolation and frustration. Securing employment presents another significant obstacle; despite possessing professional skills and experience, many immigrants encounter difficulties in having their qualifications recognized or face discrimination in the workplace. Financial hardships are prevalent, as numerous immigrants find themselves compelled to accept lower-paying jobs to make ends meet. Additionally, the intricate legal system and constantly evolving immigration policies can contribute to heightened stress and anxiety. Beyond these practical challenges lies the emotional toll of leaving family and loved ones behind, as well as the need to adapt to a new culture. Feelings of loneliness and nostalgia are common, often making it challenging to cultivate a sense of belonging. Nevertheless, immigrants are renowned for their resilience and determination. With time and support, we can surmount these obstacles and forge a successful life in the United States.

My two older daughters, Ernestine and Louise, and I arrived in the United States on December

15, 2004, on an H4 Visa, facilitated by Reverence Samuel Siebo, who was then my husband. Upon our arrival, we spent a week in Atlanta, Georgia, staying with him in his dormitory room at the Interdenominational Theological Center (ITC). Unfortunately, we could not remain there due to the limited space for the girls. Subsequently, the girls and I moved to Johnson City, Tennessee, to live with my sister-in-law, Mrs. Eliane Wilson, while Samuel completed his studies at ITC. Although we were considered legal residents in the United States, our H4 immigration status prevented us from obtaining social security numbers.

The girls were able to start school in January 2005, but I was unable to work for the same reason. To generate some income, I began braiding hair for a few people in the home we shared with my in-law. This hair braiding provided a modest income, which I shared with Samuel to assist him with gas whenever he visited us in Tennessee. Not long after, I discovered that I was pregnant with our daughter, Elaine. I affectionately refer to her as my 'Welcome to America Baby' because I became pregnant almost immediately after arriving in the country. The girls and I spent most of our time at home when they were not in school.

We attended church with my sister-in-law, Elaine, who worked nights and often returned home exhausted and in need of sleep. Some Sundays, we managed to go to church, while other times we could not due to a lack of transportation. One Sunday morning, I prepared the girls for church and waited for Sister Elaine to return from work so we could go together. However, when she arrived home, she expressed her fatigue and inability to attend. Consequently, I took the girls and we walked to a nearby Baptist church, just a ten-minute walk from my sister-in-law's apartment. As we entered the predominantly white church that morning, I felt a bit uncomfortable, but the girls were unfazed, as they were accustomed to being in a mostly white environment, given that their school was 98 percent white. That Sunday, we were warmly welcomed by the church members, who took the girls to the children's church while I remained in the sanctuary for the service.

After the church service, I was warmly greeted by the members, who were incredibly welcoming. They invited us to return, and naturally, I was eager to come back. With such great hospitality, who wouldn't want to? Among those who welcomed me was a lady who engaged me in conversation and expressed her desire to be my friend. She inquired about my living situation, and I shared that my daughters and I lived down the road in an apartment complex with my sister-in-law. She kindly offered to drive us home, and I accepted. Lisa Taylor Stephens, along with her husband Chad and their three children, took us home in their Chrysler van. This lady would later become like a sister to me. I feel that my bond with Lisa and her family was divinely orchestrated. Lisa accompanied me to nearly all my prenatal and postnatal appointments. She was the one who took me to the hospital when I was scheduled for labor induction with my daughter, Elaine.

Additionally, she would take Ernestine and Louise to her home on weekends to give me a much-needed break. Her family, including her parents, embraced my daughters and treated them with kindness.

God's guidance often arrives in unexpected forms. Much like a sculptor who transforms rough stone into a masterpiece, He navigates us through challenges and unforeseen twists to shape our character. What may initially seem like a setback can unveil hidden opportunities, and a seemingly chance encounter might introduce us to a much-needed friend. Although we may not always comprehend the journey, by placing our trust in His love and keeping our hearts open, we can discern God's mysterious hand leading us toward growth and fulfillment. My decision to walk into that church with my children was a profound act of divine intervention, and it changed everything.

After the birth of Elaine on September 30, 2005, Samuel decided it was time for us to find our own place to live. At that time, we did not have the financial means to secure an apartment, so we applied for public housing. By then, Samuel had graduated from ITC. One day, he came home from work early while Ernestine and Louise were still at school. He took baby Elaine and me to the public housing office to submit our application. We completed the application and submitted it. The officials at the public housing office informed us that the wait period was long, but since we had a young baby, they would expedite our process. While we awaited the outcome, I fell ill with gallbladder disease and was hospitalized for three weeks.

During my hospitalization, the doctor kept me on intravenous antibiotics because my gallbladder was inflamed to extend that the doctor didn't think open surgery was a good option for me at that time. Especially since I had just had a cesarean section delivery. My baby Elaine was only three weeks old when I was admitted at night, leaving Ernestine, Louise, and Elaine at home with their father and their aunt. Both Samuel and his sister had to go to work. We inquired if the doctor could allow me to keep the baby in the hospital, but that was not possible. Consequently, we needed someone to care for the children. My friend Lisa came to our aid and took Elaine to her house while Ernestine and Louise were still in school. This brought me some relief, although the two girls were saddened by my illness. Both girls struggled at school and exhibited signs of distress, prompting Louise's teacher's assistant to visit the hospital and offer to care for the girls until I was discharged. Seeing someone I didn't know come to ask about my children broke my heart, and I began to cry bitterly. This was one of the saddest moments of my life as a new immigrant in the US. Fortunately, my friend Lisa walked into my hospital room with baby Elaine. Witnessing my grief over not having anyone to care for my children, she decided to keep all three girls until I was discharged. This was a tremendous relief for me—God was truly good to me, and He still is. She cared for them for three weeks, and her family took excellent care of them.

Unmasking: A Journey Through Fear to Embrace Reality

Though trials may seem overwhelming, and shadows may lengthen, for those who walk with God, a comforting promise remains. Just as a loving parent gathers a child close in moments of fear, our Heavenly Father stands ready to intervene. When the hour of greatest need descends and we cry out in desperation, faith assures us that God's rescuing hand is near. Although the form of that rescue may not always align with our expectations, His love and protection remain constant—a beacon of hope in the darkest night.

There are truly good people in this life. Those who show kindness without seeking reward are indeed God-sent, embodying the fear of God within them. On the day of my surgery, after three weeks of antibiotic treatment, I found myself alone at my bedside. Samuel, my husband at the time, did not arrive that morning, nor did any friends. However, Pastor Donald Page, the pastor of Skyline Height Baptist Church in Johnson City, Tennessee, a friend of my friend Lisa, came to visit me in the hospital. I learned that Lisa had taken my daughters to Bible study and had asked the pastor to pray for me during my illness. Upon hearing the news, he came to find me and to pray with me the following day.

When he arrived at my room, he saw them wheeling me to the operating room, leaving him no time to pray with me. Nevertheless, he entered the room to check for anyone present but found it empty. He informed me that he sat down and said a prayer for me while I was being taken for surgery. This pastor, who was neither a relative nor my own pastor, waited for me until I emerged from surgery and returned to my room after recovery before he left.

Each time I recount this story, I become emotional, as I feel he was an angel sent by the Lord that day, conveying the message, "My daughter, you are not alone." I want everyone to understand that regardless of the situation, you are not alone. No matter what circumstances you find yourself in, the Lord is saying to you, "You are not alone." Even if you cannot see someone physically by your side, as Pastor Page was for me, know that the Lord is right there with you, ready to heal whatever pain or struggle you are facing.

My procedure was performed laparoscopically, allowing me to feel better almost immediately, and I was discharged the following day. A few days later, the public housing office contacted us for an interview and document review. It was determined that only our baby, Elaine, qualified for public housing according to their requirements. Nevertheless, they provided our family with a three-bedroom condo. We moved into this home in December 2005, right after Christmas, and we cherished our little abode.

Ernestine and Louise had to change schools, which made them unhappy as they had to leave their friends behind. However, they quickly adjusted because our new neighborhood was a low-income community with numerous programs and activities for families, especially children. There was a community center that offered an after-school program for the kids. As part of the low-income public housing program, I was required to volunteer at the community center to give back to the community. The Public Housing Authority in Johnson City mandated that any adult living in public housing who was not working or attending school must contribute volunteer hours to the community center.

I enjoyed working with the children at the center. I would place Elaine in the stroller and walk her to the community center, where I assisted younger kids with their homework and served them snacks. I committed to this three days a week from January 2006 to January 2007, until I began my Bachelor of Science in Nursing program at East Tennessee State University (ETSU) in Johnson City, Tennessee. Once I started school, I had to discontinue my volunteering at the center to focus on my studies.

CHAPTER 9

MY PATH TO ACADEMIC SUCCESS

My educational dream in the United States felt like an ocean away, especially during my time in distant Liberia. It shimmered in my mind like the American flag fluttering in travel brochures. For me, pursuing education in the US was not merely about acquiring knowledge; it represented an odyssey of independence and opportunity. In Liberia, I began my college journey at the African Methodist Episcopal University (AMEU), majoring in Religious Studies and Sociology. However, the educational experience felt different, as the curriculum was outdated and well-worn, like using an 18th-century approach to tackle 21st-century challenges. In contrast, the US promised a kaleidoscope of subjects, offering a chance to explore the esoteric and unconventional.

From Liberia, I envisioned myself in the US engaging in fiery debates in Sociology classrooms and participating in labs where groundbreaking scientific discoveries unfolded. It wasn't solely the academics that captivated me; upon my arrival in the US, I discovered a melting pot of cultures—a vibrant tapestry where my voice and unique perspective would be valued. Here, hard work and talent, rather than my family's name, could determine my success. I understood that the journey would be arduous—navigating immigration restrictions, overcoming language and accent barriers, and enduring the distance from my loved ones. Yet, the dream persisted, a constant hum beneath the surface of my daily life, balancing marriage, work, and children. It became a beacon, urging me to push boundaries and seize the future with both hands, with an American education serving as the key to unlocking a world brimming with unexplored possibilities.

Upon arriving in the United States in December 2004 with our daughter on an H4 visa, I was unable to work due to visa restrictions. Samuel and I concluded that the best course of action for me was to return to school. Before moving to the US, I was just a semester away from graduating from AMEU. My husband, Reverend Samuel Siebo, played a crucial role in encouraging me to pursue my education. However, we faced several challenges. We lacked the financial resources to cover the educational expenses, and I did not have a Social Security Number. Despite these obstacles, we prayed for guidance and asked God to intervene.

In July 2006, Samuel decided to visit East Tennessee State University (ETSU) to explore potential opportunities for me. He met with the vice president of undergraduate programs, who informed him that there were no available options for me since I did not possess a US Green Card or Permanent Resident status. However, she mentioned the possibility of a scholarship that would either pay for or waive the out-of-state fees, allowing me to pay significantly lower in-state tuition and fees.

She then referred him to the director of the college's

Gospel Choir, suggesting that I could join, and that the scholarship would cover the out-of-state fees. Samuel met with the director the same day, and after their conversation, she invited me to an audition. I was thrilled to be selected for the scholarship, marking a significant breakthrough in my educational journey. Although the scholarship covered the out-of-state tuition and fees, we were still responsible for the in-state costs. It is true that when God brings you to a challenge, He will see you through it. Miracles do happen for the children of God.

Confident in my ability to attend ETSU, I proceeded to apply to the nursing college, encouraged by several friends and inspired by my experiences in nursing care during the labor and delivery of my daughter, Elaine. I was accepted for the Spring semester of 2007. Naturally, I needed to complete the general college courses, and my acceptance into the nursing program depended on my GPA. At that time, Samuel was employed at an institution that cared for individuals with mental challenges, now known as Core Services of Northeast Tennessee. He also received a job offer from Gray United Methodist Church as an associate pastor, which he began in the Summer of 2006. Although the ETSU undergraduate program was relatively affordable, it still represented a significant expense for our income level. Nevertheless, Samuel opted for a payment plan when it was time for me to start school. During that period, I braided hair for women in the community, accepting whatever payment they could offer. I provided these hair braiding services in our apartment and occasionally in my clients' homes. Having my own professional beauty salon would have made a substantial difference.

Being accepted at ETSU was a significant achievement for me; however, due to my immigration status, I realized that I could not progress further in the program unless I regularized my status to one that would allow me to obtain a Green Card or at least a Social Security Number. To avoid dropping out of the program, we needed to find a solution. Consequently, we decided to ask our siblings, who possess their Green Cards or citizenship, to file for us. We assured them that we would cover the filing costs. Initially, we believed our siblings would be willing to assist us, but we anticipated that the challenge would be convincing them to bear the expenses. We planned to communicate that we would handle the costs ourselves. Given the alarming narratives we had encountered in the news, particularly on CNN's Lou Dobbs show regarding illegal immigrants, we felt a sense of fear. We feared that no one would want to risk their relatives or family members facing immigration troubles. Unfortunately, we received the same disappointing response from our siblings: they preferred to assist family members still in Liberia rather than help us, who were already in the U.S. This was one of the most disheartening experiences I faced, feeling abandoned by my own family during a time when I was at risk of deportation. However, upon reflection, I now understand that it was perhaps God's way of saying no. As stated in the Holy Bible, '*My glory I share with no one.*'

In that same month, my husband, Samuel Siebo,

lost his H1B status, which had allowed the girls and me to come to the United States on H4 visas. He did not share the details of what transpired, but he mentioned that the pastor who had offered him the job refused to continue with the immigration paperwork after being elevated to bishop. Consequently, he was unable to obtain his Permanent Resident Card (Green Card) because he required the pastor's approval for his I-485 application to be accepted by the United States Citizenship and Immigration Services (USCIS). As a result, he could only secure Temporary Protected Status (TPS), which was granted to all Liberians residing in the United States due to the 14 years of civil war. Unfortunately, I did not qualify for TPS either, as my arrival date in the United States was after the deadline. It's important to recognize that when God says no in any situation, He often has a better yes in store for us. At that time, we didn't fully grasp what we were asking our siblings for, and I doubt they understood either. The process of a sibling filing for another sibling's Green Card while both are in the U.S. can take up to twenty years. I needed someone with an immigration status that would allow me to obtain a Social Security number immediately, rather than waiting for an uncertain future.

After our siblings turned us down, we found ourselves with no other options, so I turned to the Internet. Often, when we face rejection from others—when they distance themselves for no apparent reason and belittle us—that's when God lifts us up right before their eyes. I began searching online for solutions to our immigration issues. While browsing, I stumbled upon information about asylum and shared it with my husband. Initially, he was hesitant. He recounted stories of many Liberians who had sought asylum in the US, only to be denied and forced to leave. This made him apprehensive about applying for asylum. With no one else to turn to, I chose to trust God and do what I could, leaving the rest in His hands. I printed the asylum application form and began writing my story, particularly my experiences during the last war in 2003. When my husband read my account, he decided to apply as well. We were unaware that two family members could not apply for asylum simultaneously. We completed our applications and mailed both packages to the designated processing office on the same date and time.

A week following the submission of our applications, I received a call from an office in Connecticut, informing me that they had a package for Samuel that had been sent to the wrong address. It turned out to be Samuel's asylum application. Meanwhile, my application was delivered to the correct address. We never understood how this mix-up occurred, but we later learned that they would not have accepted both applications anyway. I often thought it would have been better for them to accept Samuel's application instead of mine, as he is an eloquent speaker who could persuade the interviewer—something he himself acknowledged. I found myself questioning, *'Why me, Lord? Why not Samuel?'* What I failed to grasp is that God does not judge based on human standards; He sees beyond the physical and knows the beginning from the end.

In summary, my application was accepted, and I was invited for an interview in Memphis, Tennessee. Memphis was just over eight hours away from Johnson City, Tennessee, where we were living at the time. We departed Johnson City the day before my interview. After more than eight hours of driving, we arrived in Memphis just as the sun was setting. The following morning, I woke up early to prepare for the interview, and Samuel accompanied me. Upon entering the interview room, the interviewer instructed me to take a seat in front of her desk while she settled in behind it. As she slowly flipped through the pages of my application, she posed questions related to my story. I felt confident that I had answered each question flawlessly, especially as she nodded in response and seemed sympathetic to my situation. However, I was mistaken; this was merely the beginning of my journey. At the conclusion of the interview, I was informed that a decision could not be made at that office because my application had been submitted after I had been in the United States for over a year. The final decision needs to be made by a judge. Consequently, I was referred to a court for the judge to evaluate my case. I was advised to keep an eye out for a letter from the court, which would provide further instructions on the next steps.

We departed from Memphis that morning after the interview, embarking on our journey back to Johnson City. A sense of fear gripped me at the thought of having to go to court for this process. My husband, Samuel Siebo, was visibly upset and began to voice his frustrations during our drive home. *"This is why I didn't want to do this,"* he lashed out. However, we had no choice; we both needed to regularize our immigration status. In an unexpected turn of events, the senior pastor of Gray United Methodist Church, where Samuel was employed in Gray, Tennessee, learned that his Green Card application had been denied and requested that he bring his immigration paperwork. The silver lining in this situation was that once the immigration office received our applications, we were permitted to remain in the United States while awaiting a decision. Thus, we were considered legal residents during the processing of my application. All we needed to do was place our trust in God, and I did just that. I relied on Him every step of the way, engaging in fasting and prayer—I truly committed to fasting. After all, it was God who paved the way for my arrival in the United States, despite being told by three different visa counselors at the US embassy in Liberia, on five separate occasions, that I would never come to America. One counselor even advised me, *"Stop wasting your money."* Despite all that transpired, I remained steadfast in my faith. I continue to believe in the miracle-working power of God. As stated in the book of Lamentations 3:37, *"Who can speak and it happens when the Lord has not said it?"*

A week after returning home from my interview, I received a letter in the mail containing a court citation. Along with the citation, the letter included a list of immigration lawyers in the area, complete with their contact information. We reached out to those lawyers' offices immediately, but unfortunately, none of them were available for pro bono work. As a result, I had to prepare myself to attend the hearing without legal representation.

On the day of the hearing, we woke up early, secured Elaine and JoAnn in their car seats, and began our journey to Memphis. Ernestine and Louise stayed behind in Johnson City with a family friend so they could attend school. Samuel navigated using a printed MapQuest, and he did an excellent job. Although we encountered heavy traffic and numerous detours along the way, we managed to arrive without any major issues. Samuel played his gospel music CD in the car, and we both praised and worshiped God while Elaine and JoAnn entertained themselves with their toys.

After driving for about two hours, we made our first stop for a bathroom break and breakfast. We quickly grabbed our food and hopped back in the car, continuing our praise and worship. Due to the needs of the babies, we made several stops along the way. We finally arrived in Memphis around 5:00 PM that evening and checked in at the Days Inn Hotel for the night, conveniently located near the courthouse.

After settling into our hotel room, we ventured out in search of a restaurant to grab a bite to eat. The following morning, we woke up early to prepare the babies so we could head to the courthouse. This was my very first time appearing in a courtroom since arriving in the US. Upon entering, we were struck by the crowded room filled with immigrants from various countries and diverse backgrounds. Finding a seat was a challenge. We navigated through the throng and settled in the second-to-last row at the back. During my hearing, the judge was particularly stern with me that day. He called me to stand, and the proceedings unfolded as follows.

> *"Do you have legal status in the United States",* the judge asked me
> *"Yes, your honor",* I responded.
> *"What is your status,"* he asked?
> *"My husband has a TPS so I'm here on his status,"* I responded.
> *"Shut up...you don't know what you're talking about!"* He shouted.

At that moment, Elaine and JoAnn dashed through the crowded courtroom, creating a significant commotion. A multitude of immigrants awaited their hearings.

> *"Whose children are those,"* he asked?
> *"My children, your honor,"* I responded.
> He said, *"Take your children and get out of my court, and don't bring them here again. The next time you come here make sure you come with an attorney. I'm going to set another court date for you."*

The judge's actions that day only deepened Samuel's fear. I left the courtroom feeling confused and embarrassed. For more than 30 minutes, Samuel and I exchanged no words. I couldn't fathom what was going through Samuel's mind, but I was anxious and frightened, unsure of what to think. After a prolonged silence, Samuel finally cleared his throat and remarked, *"Well, we're in it now; you just have to do what you have to do."* I paused for a moment before responding, explaining that even if he denied my application, he couldn't send us out of the country because I had checked the box for withholding of removal (deportation) on my application. This sparked a conversation about our next steps and how we could find an attorney. When God brings you to it, He will see you through it. We discussed the asylum process, mapping our journey from Memphis to Johnson City. Although we were still listening to the same gospel music, we had stopped praising and worshiping. After eight hours of deliberation, we still felt uncertain about our next move, but we knew we had to wait for the court's letter regarding the next hearing date. I continued my routine of fasting and praying, trusting God for a breakthrough.

One day, Samuel and I went to Walmart to pick up some groceries for the family. As we were leaving the store, I received a call from an attorney's office in Memphis, Tennessee, inquiring about Jennifer. Samuel handed the phone to me, and the attorney informed me that he would be representing my case. I felt a sense of relief upon hearing this. I switched the phone to speaker mode so that both Samuel and I could listen to the conversation. The attorney then asked me to briefly share my story. After I explained my situation, he remarked, *"Didn't you know that you were in the U.S. for over a year before you applied for this? You have exposed yourself to law enforcement."* At this point, Samuel interjected, *"She has two American citizens."* The attorney continued, *"Do you realize how many pregnant women are waiting at the border to enter the U.S.? You are living freely without any trouble, and yet you chose to expose yourself? This doesn't look good for you, but I want you to come see me before the court hearing date."* We quickly agreed on a date to meet while still on the phone.

A few days following our conversation with the attorney, Samuel and I made a brief trip to Memphis to meet with the attorney, leaving the girls at home. During our meeting, he revealed that he had worked with the judge for some time and that the judge had personally requested him to take my case. However, he expressed doubts about the strength of my case, noting that the issue I was facing was not actively ongoing in Liberia, where we had a stable government. Additionally, having been in the United States for over a year made my case an uphill battle. He shared an intriguing story about a dream he had one night around 2:00 AM, where he conversed with another lawyer from the same court. In the dream the lawyer reassured him, saying, *"Don't worry about that case; you will win it."* As he recounted this to Samuel and me, we suggested it might have been divine intervention. He dismissed the idea, stating, "Not at all! The person I'm referring to is someone I've known for some time; he's not a good lawyer and has never won a case." Continuing our discussion, he remarked, *"If your case were about Female Genital Mutilation (FGM), that would be advantageous."* Before he could finish, Samuel chimed in, "But she had it done to her." I felt a wave of embarrassment wash over me, but Samuel seemed unfazed by my feelings. The attorney replied, *"If she has already undergone it, she can't use that as a basis for her case."* He then inquired about my daughters, to which Samuel responded, *"No, they haven't experienced that."* The attorney suggested, *"We can use your daughters instead. This way, we won't have to worry about the one-year deadline for asylum. I will withdraw your case and file for the Female Genital Mutilation (FGM) case for the girls."*

Female Genital Mutilation (FGM) is a cultural tradition that is prevalent in Liberia, referred to as Sandi Society. This practice is predominantly inflicted upon women, including middle-aged women, as well as girls and even children as young as three years old. FGM involves the partial removal of the female external genitalia, or vulva. Unfortunately, the children and young women subjected to this procedure have no say in the matter; their parents impose this practice upon them before they have the opportunity to understand their own identities. Consequently, by the time they reach an age of self-awareness, they have already lost a part of their bodies to this cruel and painful tradition. It is estimated that approximately 70 percent of women in Liberia have undergone this procedure, not out of choice, but due to cultural and parental pressures.

The attorney proceeded to withdraw my asylum application and submitted one for the girls instead. Fortunately, I did not need to write another narrative for them. On January 20, 2009, we were granted asylum. After the girls' application was submitted, we received a letter in the mail notifying us of a hearing date on the same day, coinciding with President Obama's first inauguration. During the final hearing, which was specifically for the girls' asylum case, the judge who had previously been quite harsh with me displayed a much calmer and more courteous demeanor. He called me to the stand and required me to take an oath. Given that both Ernestine and Louise were very young at the time—Ernestine was 13 and Louise was 10—they were unable to testify. Nevertheless, the judge posed a few questions to Ernestine. He then turned to me and asked, *"Will the United States citizens, Elaine and JoAnn, undergo this process if I decide to send the family back to Liberia?"* I replied, *"Yes, your honor."* To which he responded, *"Oh no."*

Following a brief legal ceremony, we were instructed to proceed to the immigration office, conveniently located near the courthouse, to obtain our asylum documents. Samuel and I were classified as derivative asylees, benefiting from our daughters' applications. At the Immigration Center, the four of us—Samuel, Ernestine, Louise, and I—received our Asylum Cards that day. We felt immense joy as we exited the immigration office with our documents in hand. Truly, what a mighty God we serve.

The asylum status we obtained granted us access to all the benefits available to US Permanent Residents and Green Card holders. We departed from Memphis early on the morning of January 21, 2009, and arrived in Johnson City that evening. Overwhelmed with joy, the eight-hour drive felt like a mere blur. Our new home radiated with joy, peace, and happiness. The following morning, I attended school, and immediately after my classes, I visited the Social Security Office to apply for my Social Security Card. *"What an exhilarating moment for me,"* I thought to myself. Once I received my Social Security Card in the mail, Samuel took me to the ETSU records office to update my Alien Registration Number to reflect my new Social Security Number.

In the spring of 2009, I entered my fifth semester at ETSU, during which I was accepted into the nursing program. My coursework included Pathophysiology and Health Assessment. Unfortunately, I ended the semester with a C minus in Pathophysiology, which was considered a failing grade for the program. This course was one of the most challenging in the nursing curriculum, taught by Dr. Masoud Ghaffari, an excellent professor known for his straightforward grading and effective teaching methods. To pass his course, students needed to earn every point possible. Although I did not achieve the required grade, I was fortunate to receive my Social Security Number, allowing me to apply for student loans to finance my education. Given my eligibility for these loans, I decided to take out a loan and retake the course during the summer to stay on track for the next semester, as I could not progress without passing. I shared my plan with Samuel, who responded, *"Yeah, I was going to talk to you about this anyway. You know that I used my retirement and all my savings to pay for your school, so we need to put it back. I will take you to the financial aid office so we can navigate the student loan process together."*

He completed the application online, and we visited the ETSU financial aid office with Elaine and JoAnn. There was a long line at the office, so I sat with the babies while Samuel stood in line and spoke with the financial counselor. He learned that I could receive all 2008 student loan awards up to the summer of 2009. Afterward, they provided him with the necessary paperwork for me to sign, which he then submitted to the counselor. It may sound unbelievable, but this is a true story. Samuel applied for all the loans I was eligible for, totaling over $37,500, and I also received a Pell Grant due to our family's low-income status. The total amount deposited into Samuel's account, including the loans and Pell Grant, exceeded $44,000 in 2009. Approximately $2,000 of this sum was allocated for my summer semester. I felt undeserving of such a significant debt, especially since we were living in government housing, where our rent and utility bills were under $250 a month. Even with the addition of his car note, our monthly expenses barely reached $500. Later, Samuel transferred to ETSU after spending a semester or two at Milligan College, where he attempted to pursue nursing. He managed to secure student loans in his own name to continue his education.

Samuel's pension, mentioned here, was money set aside for him by the United Methodist Church in Gray, Tennessee, during his time as an assistant pastor. Unbeknownst to him, this money existed. A couple of months after his termination from the church, he received a letter from the church's financial office detailing his retirement funds. Curious about the next steps, he called the office for guidance. They informed him that, despite no longer being affiliated with the church, he could leave his funds to mature. However, he opted to withdraw the money to address pressing issues, including my school fees. The total amount was approximately $6,000. Due to his early withdrawal, the Internal Revenue Service (IRS) deducted a significant portion in taxes, leaving him with about $3,500. He allocated $900 for my education and used the remainder for personal expenses.

From the spring of 2007 to the spring of 2009, Samuel spent around $10,000 on my schooling, supplemented by a small scholarship from a United Methodist Organization. I do not dispute his efforts to support my education, and I am genuinely grateful for his sacrifices. However, he often tells his audiences that he used his own money for my education, while he simultaneously took out student loans in my name, claiming he was replacing the funds he had spent on my schooling. In reality, I relied on student loans throughout my college years, and today, I carry a student loan debt of $136,651.69. Some may question why I assert that Samuel took out loans in my name when I should have been the one signing the loan agreements. My naivety allowed him to take control, and I felt compelled to maintain the relationship by remaining silent and letting him lead. This was a misguided approach for any woman in a marriage. I followed this path, and ultimately, it proved detrimental to both my children and me.

After successfully completing coursework in two

courses during the Summer Semester of 2009, I advanced to the next level in my nursing program. In the fall of 2009, I enrolled in additional nursing courses focused on the foundations of nursing. Upon passing these courses, I secured a position as a nurse assistant at Holston Medical Center. I began working at the hospital during the winter break, and when the school year commenced, I adjusted my schedule to accommodate a weekend position. Additionally, the hospital offered summer nurse externships to students who had successfully completed their foundations of nursing course. In the Summer of 2010, I applied for and was accepted into the Holston Valley Medical Center Summer Extern Program, which provided a higher pay rate than that of a regular nurse assistant. The program lasted for 10 weeks and proved to be both successful and rewarding for my nursing career, significantly enhancing my exposure to the nursing field.

Due to a change in our immigration status, we became eligible for certain government benefits, including food stamps. Our children were U.S. citizens, which further supported our application. One day, Samuel returned from work and suggested that I visit the Department of Human Services to apply for food stamps for our family. A few days later, we submitted our application. Subsequently, I received a letter requesting that I provide various documents, including financial records.

To obtain the necessary information, I took the letter to the human resources department at Holston Valley Medical Center. The representative I spoke with informed me that I was not considered an employee, as my position as a nurse extern did not qualify for employment status. Consequently, she was unable to provide me with any financial information. Instead, I used Samuel's financial details for our evaluation. We were approved for a substantial amount of food stamps. However, several months later, I received a call indicating that I had underreported our family income, which led to allegations of food stamp fraud. It turned out that the lack of information from the Holston Valley Medical Center representative had contributed to this misunderstanding.

This experience should have served as a warning against applying for or renewing food stamps, but I did not heed the lesson. Unfortunately, similar incidents occurred twice while we were still residing in Johnson City, Tennessee. During the second incident, I was uncertain about the source of the discrepancies, but Samuel provided me with his income report for the food stamp recertification. Once again, I received a call months later, informing me that I had underreported our family income, resulting in a requirement to repay the excess benefits. I ensured that we settled our debt with the state, but I became apprehensive about using the remaining balance on our food stamp card.

When Samuel was terminated from the United Methodist Church in Gray, Tennessee, some church members decided to support his family until he found another job. They came together to rent the Gray Community Center, which was conveniently located near the United Methodist Church. Samuel named the new church Faith Cathedral Ministry, which quickly gained attendance from members of Gray UMC, who were very supportive both emotionally and financially. They were able to provide Samuel with a salary, so we didn't feel the absence of the UMC too acutely. The church became our place of worship while we both completed our studies at ETSU. However, after several months, attendance began to decline as many members returned to their original churches. This shift led to a significant drop in the monthly income of Faith Cathedral Ministry. Samuel returned to work for Core Services, while I continued my job as a Pro Re Nata (PRN) nurse assistant at Holston Valley Medical Center, and we still held services at the church.

Relief and exhilaration washed over me—I had done it. The challenges that once seemed insurmountable were now conquered. This was not merely the end of a journey for me; it was the exciting beginning of a new chapter, armed with knowledge and fueled by passion. The future stretched before me, brimming with possibilities, and I was ready to embrace it.

I graduated in May 2011 from ETSU. Following my graduation, I secured a nursing position at the Johnson City Medical Center through the recommendation of my friend Janet Gar. Although I had not yet passed the State Board, I was able to start orientation immediately. I was thrilled about my new job, and we were grateful that our family now had an income, allowing us to buy a home and move out of public housing.

Samuel and I began searching for a home in the Johnson City area and visited several properties. However, it proved challenging to find the type of home we desired due to our rental history. At that time, we were still living in public housing, paying around $165.00 in rent, while looking at homes priced between $250,000 and $275,000. We faced multiple rejections. One banker later informed us that to qualify for the homes we were interested in, we needed to have a solid income history for three years. She advised us to leave public housing and rent a private apartment, which would help us establish a better rental payment record. We considered this advice but ultimately, could not execute it as Samuel was again terminated from his job.

A few weeks later, after our conversation with the banker, Samuel was fired from his job at Core Services in early July 2011. This prompted him to express a desire to leave Johnson City. He mentioned that someone had told him about a hospital chaplain training position in Columbia, South Carolina. He applied for the job and was called for an interview in mid-July. The family made a quick trip to South Carolina for Samuel's interview. During that trip, I contacted the Palmetto Health Human Resources office to inquire about registered nurse positions for new graduates. The representative informed me she would check and get back to me if any positions were available. Within an hour, she called back to say there were openings and wanted to schedule an interview with me the following day if I was interested. Following Samuel's lead, I expressed my interest and attended the interview on July 12, 2011. After the interview, they extended an offer to me. Samuel was also accepted for the hospital chaplaincy training, which was a paid program. With both of us assured of jobs in South Carolina, we decided to search for a home there. We aimed to move into our own home upon relocating, rather than renting. Samuel reached out to a realtor in South Carolina, and we made several visits to view homes. Unfortunately, we faced obstacles again, as we needed to have worked in the state and provide at least three months of pay stubs to qualify for the loan we were pursuing.

CHAPTER 10

WHAT IS THE CHRISTIAN CHURCH FEAR?

During my early journey with the AME Church in Liberia, I gained significant insights about the church. In March 2000, I was elected as the Young People's Division (YPD) Director of the AME Church in Liberia. This election coincided with Bishop Adam J. Richardson's final Annual Conference in Liberia and marked the end of his term as bishop of the 14th Episcopal District. During this period, the Women's Missionary Society (WMS) of the Liberia Annual Conference of the African Methodist Episcopal Church also elected their core officers. As the YPD Director, I was a member of the WMS, responsible for overseeing YPD activities and reporting to the WMS. To familiarize myself with my role, I consistently read the AME Church Doctrine and Discipline.

At that time, the AME Church in Liberia had only one Annual Conference—the Liberia Annual Conference. I served under the late Bishop Richard Franklin Norris, who was the bishop of the 14th Episcopal District. I brought my AME Discipline to every WMS meeting and YPD function as a safeguard against any controversies that might arise. My knowledge of the Discipline guided my behavior and interactions within the church. However, my husband Samuel often found himself at odds with church leadership, which led to discontent among WMS leaders regarding my involvement. I frequently felt sidelined and marginalized in my role as YPD Director during events. In a retaliatory move, the WMS president publicly disrobed me during our 2000 weekend retreat in Buchanan, Grand Bassa County, Liberia.

During that event, my responsibilities as the YPD Director were temporarily assigned to another individual who carried out my duties in my presence. I promptly referenced the AME Discipline, asserting my right to fulfill my role as YPD Director. My insistence, however, was met with disapproval from the friends of the WMS president. Fortunately, the late Mrs. Kuler Brapoh came to my defense, instructing the president to allow me to perform my duties as outlined in the AME Discipline. Following this experience in Buchanan, I felt a deep gratitude for the AME Church's Doctrine and Discipline. However, I regretfully did not take the time to read the book of Discipline in its entirety, a shortcoming that would later affect my experiences with church leadership in the United States.

During a conversation with Samuel, he recounted stories about bishops in the AME Church who divorce their wives and remarry women they believe could help them ascend to higher positions within the church. I cannot recall what prompted this discussion or why he chose to share it with me, but I found it hard to believe that the church would permit such actions within the Body of Christ. I assumed it was just one of Samuel's many anecdotes and did not take it seriously. However, one of the bishops he mentioned was the late Bishop Richard

Franklin Norris, who was an active bishop at the time. Samuel claimed that Bishop Norris divorced his first wife and married a woman who worked in a bishop's office to advance his ambitions of becoming a bishop. He then asked me, *"Do you see how successful Bishop Norris is in the church today?"* It was true; Bishop Norris was a highly successful and influential leader in the AME Church. He played a significant role in helping Samuel and many other Liberian ministers thrive in their ministerial careers in the United States. Aware of Bishop Norris's past and his achievements, Samuel decided to emulate his path. He devised a plan to divorce me and abandon his family.

Bishop Jeffery Leath articulated a significant point in one of his posts on Facebook: *"Clergy and Lay Leaders are mirroring the styles of the bishop. It is hypocritical to critique negative features in 'them' while practicing them yourselves. This also explains why reform has been slow and difficult. No one wants to make accountability at the top essential because they do not want to be accountable at the middle and bottom."* He further emphasized in another post, *"The bishops do it, is a poor response to unethical behavior! One of the reasons wrong attitudes and bad habits permeate our Zion is that the folk imitate the folk at the top. They are not so quick to reform when they benefit from the same behavior at every level of the church...in every component. Bishops' wrong actions are no justification for clergy wrongdoing. Clergy errors are not an excuse for misjudgments."* I resonate with

Unmasking: A Journey Through Fear to Embrace Reality

Bishop Leath's perspective that, as Christians, we should not emulate the negative actions of others, regardless of their apparent success. However, I also believe that churches and Christian organizations must establish rules and regulations to prevent the intentional and un-Christian behaviors exhibited by those in leadership.

Leaders hold positions of influence, and "with that influence comes responsibility." They must serve as good examples for those they influence. As stated in Proverbs 22:6, parents are encouraged to *"bring up their children in the way they should go, and when they are old, they will not depart from it."* This underscores the importance of the church carefully examining who they choose as their leaders.

The issue of dishonesty within the Christian Church is both complex and multifaceted. Although the core teachings of Christianity advocate for truth and honesty, the institution has unfortunately been marred by instances of deception and manipulation throughout its history. Leaders, including my former husband Samuel Siebo, have exploited the Christian Church for their own selfish purposes. The ramifications of this dishonesty are extensive, encompassing individual acts of lying and financial misconduct, as well as broader concerns such as historical revisionism and the suppression of dissenting voices. Such instances of dishonesty can undermine trust within the church and tarnish its reputation, necessitating introspection and a renewed commitment to the values of truth and transparency.

To my utmost surprise, my husband Samuel filed for divorce and was granted the decree in my absence. The next thing I knew, his wedding photos began flooding my Facebook Messenger from various individuals. Some sent them as a form of teasing or mockery, while others offered them in solidarity. I understood that friends and family often identify with those going through such experiences. At that time, I wasn't seeking sympathy or patronizing gestures for my divorce. Instead, I was hoping to witness a church that truly embodies the principles of Christianity—unfortunately, that did not happen. In that moment, I longed to see a Christian Church that stands firm on biblical teachings.

I questioned why a man or woman aspiring to hold the esteemed office of bishop in the Christian faith would abandon their family and enter into another relationship without an explanation. Instead, I witnessed a troubling side of the church. I saw bishops, pastors, officers, and members of the AME Church celebrating a man who had cast aside his family to marry another woman he met during his campaign for bishop. I observed the church applauding a man who forsook his wife and young children, all while pursuing a campaign to become a bishop. I even saw the church celebrating a man whose 14-year-old daughter was led to deny the existence of God. Where is the Christian morality being taught within the church? The AME Church was established in response to what was deemed an 'ungodly act or treatment' in the White Methodist Church. I found myself asking, 'Where is the godly treatment in the Black Methodist Church?' I have been searching for the embodiment of Christian values within the AME Church, and I continue to seek it. I hope to find it one day, but it seems the church may harbor an inherent fear of being exposed for its misdeeds.

To begin with, Samuel Siebo and I are both members of the AME Church. He was pastor for several years and then he later became a Chaplain in the United States Army representing the AME Church in the military. He was deployed to Afghanistan in less than a year when he became an Active-Duty chaplain. While in Afghanistan, he decided that he wanted to run for the office of a Bishop in the AME Church. I was a bit concerned when he told me about his plan to run for the bishopric position because prior to his deployment he promised to help run a campaign for one of the lead pastors in Columbia South Carolina who was running for the office of a bishop. We attended this pastor's church almost every Sunday. Therefore, it was kind of embarrassing when Samuel decided to run for the office of a bishop. Especially when he had promised to help with the pastor's campaign. Another concern was that I personally didn't think that Samuel was ready to serve as a bishop—he was not matured spiritually and ready to lead as a Bishop.

To me, this office of bishop should be a highly spiritual position that requires a lot of self-discipline, maturity, self-awareness, and humbleness according to 1st Timothy chapter 3. As a wife, I knew that Samuel did not have those qualities. He's a hard worker and he knows how to make connections. Being a bishop is not something he would do well at this time if the church was looking for spiritual leaders—Samuel was not a spiritual man. He had a worldly mindset—the spirit of God did not reside within him.

At times, I found myself needing to remind Samuel about his identity and how he navigates challenges within our home and among his siblings. However, when I attempted to persuade him to pause his campaign and assist the pastor, whom he had promised to support, he insisted that the Lord had instructed him to run for the position of bishop while he was in Afghanistan. I often questioned, *"What Lord?"* Consequently, I urged him to inform the pastor of his intentions before making any public announcements about his campaign. He agreed to this suggestion and later informed me that he had spoken with the pastor, who appeared to have no objections to his candidacy. I then reflected, *"If the Lord has indeed spoken to my husband about becoming a bishop, who am I to obstruct his path?"*

While Christianity upholds the principles of honesty and truthfulness, the Church's history is regrettably marred by instances of dishonesty—such as those exhibited by my former husband, Samuel Siebo. Treachery and an individual's overwhelming ambition to achieve their desires can manifest in various ways, ranging from personal acts of deceit within congregations to larger scandals involving infidelity, financial mismanagement, abuse of power, and the concealment of wrongdoing. These acts of dishonesty not only tarnish the Church's reputation but also erode the fundamental values of the Christian faith, fostering disillusionment and mistrust among believers. During my harrowing experience of continuous abuse and manipulation at the hands of a Bishop wannabe, Samuel Siebo faced no repercussions from the Church, which was aware of my suffering.

CHAPTER 11

2ND CAMPAIGNS FOR BISHOP AND CHURCH'S LEADERS DECEPTIONS

Every day, I find myself pondering the question, *"Was I under some sort of spell from my husband Samuel Siebo?"* This reflection often arises in the wake of his defeat for the position of Bishop in 2016. As a devoted wife, I felt compelled to support my husband, Samuel Siebo, in his campaign for the Bishop of the AME Church. I dedicated extra hours to raise funds for campaign materials and travel expenses. Our campaign journeys varied; sometimes the entire family joined us, while other times it was just the two of us. Running a campaign proved to be quite costly, yet we navigated the process successfully by collaborating closely. Unfortunately, despite our efforts, he was not elected as bishop during his first attempt in 2016. Consequently, we embarked on the campaign journey once more three years later, as the AME Church prepared to elect new bishops and general officers.

In 2019, Samuel and I embarked on his second campaign rotation, beginning with the AME Church General Board and Bishop Council meeting in June in Alabama. Following that, we attended the Lay Organization Convention from June to July in Bellevue, Washington. The Women's Missionary Society Quadrennial Convention of the AME Church took place in Columbus, Ohio, from July to August. Unbeknownst to me, it was during this convention that Samuel decided to divorce me.

The overseas bishops of the AME Church frequently assume the roles of overseas district delegates for voting purposes during various conferences. In my view, this practice is neither legal nor required by the church; bishops should not replace absentee delegates with arbitrary individuals. Nevertheless, this has been an ongoing practice for years, often conducted discreetly, and it appears that no one has raised concerns about it. Consequently, this has become the norm within the church, reflecting a troubling lack of accountability. This issue is a growing concern and is currently the subject of ongoing discussions within the church. Notably, approximately 85% of the overseas delegates elected to attend conferences are unable to obtain visas, leading bishops in those districts to fill their positions with random individuals.

When Samuel and I decided to attend the Women's Conference in Ohio, he asked Bishop McCloud, a friend of his, to include me in the Liberian delegation. The bishop agreed; however, for some reason, the registration deadline was altered from the usual church protocol. It was conducted online ahead of time, prior to the convention's start date. Consequently, I was unable to register for the position the bishop had assigned to me. Shortly before the WMS election date, one of the ladies from the Liberian delegation chose to withdraw. As a result, Samuel suggested that I use this young lady's name tag to cast my vote. This situation was both problematic and embarrassing for me, as Samuel is well-known in the church, and many people recognized me as his wife, given that I often accompanied him to these conferences. I understood that bishops typically fill positions for overseas delegates who cannot attend the conference, but this was a different scenario, especially since I would have to use someone else's name tag. I felt uncomfortable and embarrassed about this, but Samuel interpreted my refusal to use the name tag as a lack of support for his campaign. Despite my ongoing support for him, he developed a negative attitude towards me. He did not speak to me from the day of the WMS election until our trip back home. He accused me of blocking his opportunity, claiming that he had promised those running for the WMS position that he would secure votes for them in exchange for their support during the general conference. By refusing to vote for them, he believed I had jeopardized his chances of winning the election for bishop.

While we were still at the conference in Ohio, he confided in his brother, who was with us, that he intended to file for divorce as soon as he returned home. I had no idea that he had been contemplating a divorce long before the AME Convention. Upon returning home on August 3, 2019, Samuel filed for divorce just two days later, as indicated by the date on the document. I found myself questioning, *'Was my failure to vote using another person's name a legitimate reason for his divorce, or was there something more?'* I struggled to accept the reality of the divorce, as I believed I had done nothing to justify it. However, when the enemy (the devil) seeks to destroy you, he often exploits the smallest issues to bring you down.

Before filing for his divorce, we had raised funds and resources for Samuel to travel to South Africa to campaign for the position of bishop of the AME Church. He believed that South Africa had the largest delegation on the African continent attending the AME Conferences. Consequently, he decided to make multiple campaign trips there to persuade many delegates to vote for him. However, during his campaign in South Africa, he encountered a girl he fell in love with. Samuel Siebo viewed this as a significant opportunity to become a bishop by marrying a South African woman. He believed that marrying a South African would encourage the delegates to vote for him as their in-law. To achieve this, he felt compelled to find a way to divorce me, his legal wife in the United States, so he could remarry his South African girlfriend. This was a dishonorable approach for a minister of the gospel to abandon his spouse while still holding a high position. For me, it was deeply shameful and an affront to the Church of God. Unfortunately, the leaders in the AME Church who were aware of Samuel's intentions did nothing to prevent him from destroying his family.

I have been a member of the AMEC since my teenage years, but it was through my divorce that I truly understood the moral standards of the AME church regarding marriage and family. When Samuel filed for divorce, I felt a mix of fear and embarrassment about sharing our situation with my family and friends. Many of them had anticipated this outcome, yet I was unwilling to accept that he would take such a step against me. Consequently, I aimed to keep them completely uninformed while seeking others who could intervene—I desperately wanted to save my marriage.

I reached out to his mother and one of his brothers, but they advised me to consult a lawyer and have them respond to the case, suggesting that this would stall the process. They believed that once the proceedings were delayed, the family would have sufficient time to communicate with him. After considering their advice, I decided to approach the Army Chaplaincy for assistance. I spoke with a leader of the chaplains at Fort Riley, who informed me that there was little they could do since it was a civil matter. He recommended that my best course of action would be to consult a civilian lawyer.

Following my conversation with the Army Chaplain, I noticed that Samuel was no longer pastoring the Army Gospel Service on the base. Although my intention was never to get him into trouble, I was merely seeking help to preserve my marriage and keep my family intact. In my opinion, the military made the right decision by suspending him from his pastoral duties. Church leaders must maintain stability in their personal lives to uphold their leadership roles. A pastor should not jeopardize their family based on personal feelings and then continue in their pastoral responsibilities.

Since I was unable to get the Army chaplaincy to intervene, I decided to heed the advice of Samuel's mother and brother by hiring a lawyer, though that did not prove helpful either. After engaging the lawyer, I submitted all the documents I had received from the court. The lawyer responded to the petition, and the divorce process commenced. After several court hearings and still seeking assistance, I chose to consult a church leader to explore potential help, especially since we played a significant role in the church and my husband was campaigning for a high office within it. When I informed Samuel of my efforts to save our marriage, he retorted, *"You just want to air our business so other people can start meddling in it."* Contrary to his assertion, I had no intention of exposing our issues. I told him that I would reach out to Bishop McCloud, his friend, if that was his preference. He agreed, so I contacted Bishop McCloud and candidly expressed my need for his assistance in salvaging our marriage. During our discussion, I recounted the events that transpired during the Convention, particularly my refusal to wear the tag of one of his delegates from Liberia to vote at the WMS Convention. The bishop responded, *"Do you realize that what you are sharing could jeopardize our friendship?"* It resonates with the truth in Bishop Leath's statement to the AMEC Reform Group that *"Friendship"* is detrimental to our church! We tend to overlook wrongdoing, create positions, show bias, and grant privileges to *"Friends."*

I informed the bishop that Samuel was aware of my conversation with him. He then inquired, *"Where is he now?"* I replied that Samuel had moved out of the house. After that phone call with the bishop, I never heard from him again. Regardless of whether he spoke with Samuel about the situation, he completely cut off communication with me. While I was trying to save our marriage from ruin, the divorce proceedings continued. After several hearings, my lawyer informed me that she could no longer represent me due to my inability to pay her fees. In contrast, Samuel had agreed to cover her fees and part of our daughter's student loans in exchange for our properties in South Carolina and Liberia. This was particularly disheartening, as I had already exhausted all my savings to pay my legal fees. Upon hearing this from my lawyer, I felt devastated. During one of our discussions, I had expressed my need to secure the home in South Carolina so that my daughters and I could return and attend their former school. She had assured me that she would fight for me to obtain the family home. Unfortunately, the only assistance she provided during the divorce proceedings was securing an emergency order for my daughters and me to remain in the military quarters, and for Samuel to provide support until the divorce was finalized.

During one of my visits to my lawyer's office to discuss divorce issues, she mentioned that she had advised Samuel's lawyer to encourage him to cease his coercive actions towards me regarding the case. She claimed that Samuel had told his lawyer he doubted I would use the term 'coercion' because I was unfamiliar with such terminology. Additionally, I was not well-versed in the American legal system. In reality, I had not used the word 'coercion' at all. I had merely shared some text messages I received from Samuel and recounted a phone conversation we had. However, my lawyer understood the implications of those communications and chose to advise Samuel accordingly. Following her discussion with Samuel and his lawyer, she seemed to favor Samuel, likely because she anticipated he would be able to pay her fees, given my unemployment status. She assumed I would not have the financial means to afford her services. The only feedback I received from her after our conversation was that Samuel would not agree, or that she did not want Richard, Samuel's lawyer, to give her a hard time. By that point, she had recognized my inexperience with the U.S. legal system, especially since Samuel had already informed her of my vulnerabilities. Consequently, she decided to abandon my case and pursue her payment from Samuel.

At that moment, I had no time to worry about my lawyer or how I would raise funds for attorney fees. Instead, I decided to reach out to another lead pastor from the AME Church, who is Samuel's best friend and also hails from Liberia. I explained my situation to him, and he assured me that he would speak to Samuel to understand what was happening. A day or two later, he called to inform me that Samuel had made up his mind and would not change it for anything. I appreciated his willingness to provide feedback on my request for intervention, unlike the bishop, who had remained silent up to that point.

What troubled me was that after Samuel's relationship became public on Facebook, this pastor unfriended me and then became friends with Samuel's new partner. Subsequently, he began to support Samuel publicly. I cannot fathom his reasons for this shift, but he consistently posted motivational comments on Samuel's Facebook posts, suggesting that it is acceptable for a pastor to divorce their spouse without cause and pursue another relationship even before the divorce is finalized. Such behavior is concerning, as it could lead other Christians away from the teachings of God. The book of Galatians, Chapter 6:1-3, clearly outlines the responsibilities of believers.

The founding history of the AME Church indicates that it emerged in response to what its members describe as *"Unchristian Practices."* Given this background, one might expect the AME Church to exemplify a high standard of core Christianity, adhering closely to Biblical principles. Bishop Leath, in a post directed at AME reformers on Facebook, stated, *"The AME Church believes that lying, stealing, adultery, hypocrisy, abuse of the body, and oppression are contrary to the will of God."* I resonate with Sidney Williams' response to this post, which highlighted that *"doctrinal statements are helpful, but cognitive dissonance arises when our actions contradict our professed beliefs."* During my divorce, an AME church leader remarked, *"I understand that what your husband Rev. Siebo did is wrong, but the church lacks any law that prohibits his actions, and I have my family to support. I cannot allow anyone to jeopardize my livelihood and that of my family."* This raises a critical question: why does the church not establish moral standards for its leaders, particularly those in spiritual positions? 1 Timothy chapter 3 outlines the qualifications for church leaders, detailing the character traits necessary for someone to be appointed as a bishop.

Being Christlike requires more than merely identifying as a Christian. As Bishop Leath stated, *"What good is Lenten reflection if all we do is rationalize sin and errors?"* As followers of Christ Jesus, we must be prepared to embrace discomfort in order to advance His agenda within our community, church, school, and family. Commitment to doing God's will is essential for the building of His kingdom. We read about early Christians who stood firm in their convictions for the sake of kingdom building. They willingly exposed themselves, and through their courage, prophecies were fulfilled. Shadrach, Meshach, and Abednego exemplified this by refusing to conform to societal pressures for the sake of their faith (Daniel 3). They faced what appeared to be a perilous situation, designed by the enemy to humiliate them into denying their God. Yet, their bravery brought honor to God's name. As children of the Most High God, we too must be willing to confront what seems dangerous in the pursuit of righteousness.

Time and again, some churches have let down their congregations in various ways. This failure can manifest through the abuse of power, prioritizing wealth and expansion over the needs of their members, or harboring harmful ideologies that exclude or discriminate against certain groups. The actions of the leadership in the AME Church where I grew up were unfathomable and un-Christian. This hurtful behavior, predominantly among male leaders, must be addressed to prevent leading the flock astray. Furthermore, churches can fail by neglecting the spiritual and emotional well-being of their members. Focusing solely on rituals and traditions, without fostering genuine connection and support, is misguided. In the most egregious cases, churches can even become complicit in acts of violence or oppression, further betraying the trust and safety that their members seek.

CHAPTER 12

You are a Survival, and Not a Victim

When faced with hatred, it is essential to maintain composure and self-control. The first step is to pause and take deep breaths, ensuring that you do not react impulsively, as this can escalate the situation. Recognize that the hatred directed at you often arises from the other person's issues, insecurities, or misunderstandings, rather than anything inherently wrong with you. Strive to maintain empathy and compassion, understanding that their behavior reflects their inner turmoil. It is beneficial to establish clear boundaries, asserting your right to be treated with respect, and if necessary, distancing yourself from toxic individuals. Engage in open, non-confrontational communication when the situation permits, expressing your feelings calmly and seeking to understand their perspective. However, do not feel obligated to change their mind or justify your existence; your worth is not determined by their approval. Seek support from friends, family, or professionals who can provide guidance and reinforce your self-worth. Remember to prioritize your mental health through activities that bring you peace and joy, such as exercise, hobbies, or mindfulness practices. Reflect on the experience as an opportunity for growth, becoming stronger and more resilient. Lastly, always prioritize your safety; if the hatred escalates to harassment or threatens your well-being, do not hesitate to seek legal assistance or involve authorities. By managing your response thoughtfully, you can navigate through hate with dignity and preserve your emotional well-being.

As an individual, you possess the power to shape your own narrative when confronted with internal adversaries. You can emerge from what may feel like your darkest nightmares with a smile on your face, leaving your foes perplexed by your resilience in the face of adversity. Alternatively, you might choose to succumb to despair, allowing your enemies to take pleasure in your suffering. Regardless of the challenges you face, remember that God is always present in the storm, guiding you through. To thwart the schemes of the enemy, all it requires is courage and self-motivation. You are not a victim. Often, what your adversaries intended for harm, God can transform into a blessing for your benefit and for His glory.

Often, when people have wronged you, they anticipate a negative response in return. This is why it is crucial to forgive those who have hurt you; your forgiveness becomes a burden for them to bear. They will live in fear of your potential retaliation, unable to comprehend that you could forgive their grievous actions. It's important to recognize that individuals respond to fear in various ways. Some may react with arrogance and deceit, while others may respond with humility. There are those who will never take responsibility for their actions. When someone harms you and speaks about you arrogantly, do not dignify their behavior with a negative reaction. Their words stem from fear of the consequences of their actions against you. As a child of God, it

Unmasking: A Journey Through Fear to Embrace Reality

is essential to understand that this behavior is not new to humanity. History and scripture teach us that nothing occurring today is unprecedented. You may be facing these challenges for the first time in your life, but that does not mean you are the first to endure such experiences. Rather, it signifies that this situation is part of your journey toward fulfilling your destiny. Consider the story of Joseph in the Bible, specifically in Genesis chapter 50, and observe how grievously his brothers treated him. Witness how he triumphed over their evil schemes, overpowering darkness in a manner that it could not comprehend the light within him. Joseph made every effort to demonstrate to his brothers that he had forgiven them for their wrongdoing, yet they struggled to believe that he could forgive them so easily. Their fear of his potential vengeance was evident, as they resorted to deceit, claiming that their late father Jacob had instructed them to ask for his forgiveness for the evil they had committed against him.

Sometimes, it can be beneficial to let your enemies dwell in uncertainty about whether you will retaliate. Allow them to live in that fear. As a person of faith who values peace and God, it is wise to forgive your enemies and move on, for they will remain trapped in the nightmares of their own making. Let them grapple with their guilt for having wronged you. Consider Joseph, who thrived and prospered while his brothers were consumed by fear, haunted by their past misdeeds. Your enemies will always reflect on their actions, and if you grant them the chance, they may attempt to harm you repeatedly, or even seek to destroy you. This is especially true when they believe they have defeated you. However, when they look back and see that you are still standing strong, it can be a powerful reminder of resilience.

Upon reflection, I often marvel at the goodness of God and His miraculous powers. During our divorce, my husband took everything we had accumulated over our 21 years of marriage, boasting about it to family and friends. His lies and dishonesty throughout the proceedings led to my homelessness. With excitement, he shared with his loved ones that he had secured everything we built together as a couple, leaving me with nothing after the divorce. He felt a sense of pride in his actions, viewing it as a significant victory for himself—but we serve a just God. While I worked tirelessly to support our family during his military career preparations, he was devising malicious plans against me. He coerced me into quitting my job to follow him on his military assignment, only to later seek a divorce driven by his lustful desires—desires that would ultimately reveal his true character to the world.

No one who harms those who depend solely on God will escape unpunished. Yes, he took everything from me, as he claimed, but he could not strip away the integrity of God. He was unaware that the God who sees and knows all things, the prayer-answering God, the judge of all judges, and the ultimate vindicator, was poised to execute justice in His own time and season, humbling him and exposing him to the world. Human beings may manipulate systems for their selfish gain, but they cannot manipulate the integrity of God. God is a God of integrity, and He does not show favoritism based on titles. He will reveal Himself when the time is right. Often, we may feel like victims of our own making, particularly our emotional struggles, but in truth, we are not. People sometimes entice us into becoming victims of our heart's desires. While our enemies may want us to feel that way, we are, in fact, survivors of their misguided hatred. Although I experienced frustration transitioning from a five-bedroom modern home that I worked hard to acquire to living in an unfinished basement, I never wavered. I continued to pursue my goals. In those moments, I felt bitterness and self-loathing for allowing myself to endure such hardship. I was hurt, filled with anguish and pain. However, I soon realized that anger, unforgiveness, bitterness, and hatred were merely tools for the enemy to hinder me from receiving God's glory.

As I sat in that dimly lit basement room one night, tears streaming down my cheeks, I resolved to console myself. I began to speak to myself as if someone else were offering me comfort. The first thing I said, calling my own name, was, *"Jennifer, it could have been worse. Aren't you grateful that you are still able to move around well?"* Then I posed a crucial question: *"How can you cling to anguish, bitterness, self-pity, and unforgiveness while expecting God to answer your prayers?"* After a few moments of reflection, the answer to this question marked a sobering realization and became a source of inspiration for letting go. I affirmed to myself, *"God must be God in my life."* I wanted all people to be liars, but for God to be true in my life. Letting go is challenging, especially when others have hurt you deeply. However, how can you expect God to respond to your prayers if you refuse to forgive? Do not be the one to carry the burdens of your enemies. Forgive them and do not let their opinions of you weigh you down. Often, what others say about you is inconsequential; what truly matters is what you say about yourself. Allow them to live in constant fear of your return, knowing that you have already forgiven them.

Before my life took a downward turn due to Samuel filing for divorce, my husband Samuel was selected to become a U.S. Army Chaplain. He completed his training and served overseas for several months while I remained in the U.S. caring for our children. Upon his return from Afghanistan, he was assigned to Fort Bliss in El Paso, Texas. With this new assignment, he preferred that the family not relocate with him. Consequently, he decided that the girls and I would stay in our home in South Carolina, as he intended to request an assignment closer to us. Within a few months, he was assigned to Fort Jackson in South Carolina. Meanwhile, I continued to work in South Carolina until January 2019, when the family relocated with Samuel to Fort Riley in Kansas for his military assignment. While in Kansas, my husband filed for divorce in August and moved out of military housing, leaving me and the girls behind.

According to the court order, I had to turn over Samuel Siebo's military home to him by February

2, 2020, so he could move back in with Elaine and JoAnn. I left Kansas at 4:00 AM on that date. At the time, I had been out of work for about a year due to my relocation with him, making it challenging to secure a rental property because of my work history. Unable to find a rental, my cousin Yar Davay and her husband kindly agreed to take me and my mother, who was still living in South Carolina, into their home in Ohio. While still in Kansas, I applied for multiple jobs, including one with Ohio Health in Columbus. I received two job offers: one in Kansas and another with Ohio Health. I chose to accept the position in Ohio, even though it paid less, as I had no place to stay in Kansas and did not know anyone there. In Ohio, however, I would be surrounded by familiar faces.

The drive from Kansas to Columbus, Ohio, took over 12 hours. I was determined to work and find a place for my children to live with me. Upon arriving in Columbus, I began work the following week. Before my move to Ohio, my mother had traveled from South Carolina to be with my cousin Yar and her family, as I could not afford to pay for her apartment in South Carolina after my husband had kicked her out of our home. Therefore, when I arrived in Ohio, my mother was already there, staying in the one-bedroom space that Yar and her husband had provided for us. To ensure some privacy, I requested to stay in their basement while my mother occupied the bedroom. I sought a quiet area for my prayer time, wanting to spend more time with the Lord in prayer. They graciously agreed to my request, and I stayed in the basement for a little over two months before finally securing a rental home.

Letting go of my hurt was one of the best decisions I ever made for myself. Soon, everything began to fall into place. The moment I released my pain, God blessed me with approval for a three-bedroom condo for rent, just a month after starting my new job. I transitioned from living in a basement to my own rented home, where my daughters joined me. I found peace within myself, knowing I had a place to call home. I communicated with Samuel whenever necessary, despite his persistent anger and reluctance to engage with me or the girls. He became verbally abusive over the phone, but I recognized that his behavior stemmed from fear and guilt—fear that I would seek revenge for the pain he caused me. Those who inflict harm on others without remorse become ensnared in their own web of lies. They fabricate stories and eventually start to believe their own falsehoods, refusing to take responsibility for their actions. Although Samuel Siebo took everything we had worked for in the US and the assets we acquired in Liberia over the years, I turned to God for justice. I never ceased praying for Him to fight my battles.

After Samuel Siebo was arrested by law enforcement officers and incarcerated on charges of molestation and the rape of his own daughter, his first instinct was to concoct a narrative that would convince others of his innocence. He attempted to shift the blame onto me, portraying me as the architect of his downfall. In his eyes, I became the embodiment of evil. The devil, as we know, is cunning, and it is crucial for us to remain vigilant against his schemes. Once we, as believers, recognize the devil's tricks, we can effectively counteract the strategies he employs to undermine us.

While in jail, he reached out to his brothers, instructing them to contact anyone connected to me and spread the falsehood that *"Jennifer has manipulated the girls into lying about me to law enforcement, claiming that I molested my daughter when she was 15 years old, and now I'm in jail. Let them know that Jennifer is responsible for my incarceration."* At that time, I was completely unaware of his arrest. When I eventually received messages from his brother and several other family members informing me of his situation, I felt a wave of disappointment and frustration towards the man I had once married. However, as I reflected on the underlying motives behind their messages and considered the source, I resolved not to let it affect me. I recognized that he was attempting to provoke a reaction from me, hoping to pressure me into persuading our daughter to withdraw her case against him in court. This was precisely what those who contacted me suggested I do. Although he was well aware that the allegations were not new, he remained convinced that I was seeking revenge. He was left to navigate his legal troubles with assistance from influential members of the AME Church, who served as character witnesses on his behalf.

I have chosen to forgive you, my dear ex-husband. I refuse to carry the burdens of bitterness, anger, hatred, and unforgiveness. I have come to realize that forgiveness is a powerful weapon that the enemy cannot withstand; it causes them to fall into their own traps. As they continue to set more traps for themselves, they will find that when one strategy intended to bring you down fails, they will attempt to devise another. The more they try to hurt you, the worse their situation becomes. This is because they will only entangle themselves further in their own schemes. God will allow you to witness their actions and uncover their malicious plans.

When Samuel's initial strategy failed to achieve his desired outcome, he devised other plans. His brother traveled to Liberia to meet with our daughter's biological mother. To enlist her support, they aimed to convince her that I was also a witch. They wanted her to believe that I had bewitched her daughter, rendering her ineffective among her siblings. They overlooked the fact that molestation and rape can lead to severe mental health issues, which may adversely affect the victim for an extended period, if not for life, if left untreated.

During that time, I was told that Samuel's brother traveled to Liberia and told our daughter's mother, *"I came to inform you that your daughter is struggling in America. The wicked woman my brother married has bewitched her."* He continued, *"Only your daughter is thriving. Can you believe that she isn't working? I just want you to know that heaven helps those who help themselves."* In Liberia, the phrase *"Heaven helps those who help themselves"* is often used as encouragement by those who believe in voodoo power, seeking it as a solution to their problems.

It is crucial to recognize that the devil tirelessly attempts to bring down God's children. As one attack fails, he launches another until he finds a way to destroy a person. However, he cannot prevail against God's children if they believe in and understand the miraculous power of their Lord. Those who know their God will be strong and perform great deeds, while those who act wickedly against God's covenant will be corrupted by flattery, as stated in Daniel 11:32.

Following the failure of my ex-husband's brother, Samuel Siebo took it upon himself to contact the mother of our daughter. He claimed that I was a witch and accused me of bewitching her daughter to falsely implicate him to law enforcement. Furthermore, he pressured her to persuade her daughter to withdraw the case from court, threatening that she would encounter serious repercussions with law enforcement if she did not comply, despite the existence of a restraining order that prohibited him from any third-party contact with her. The entire conversation was recorded.

The enemy often becomes ensnared in their own quest to harm others. Believers in our Lord Jesus Christ, who maintain clarity of mind despite being wronged, frequently allow the Lord to fight their battles to the very end. Do not be afraid or attempt to interfere in this struggle, for the battle is not yours, as stated in 2 Chronicles 20:15.

This is how God desires us to be when we entrust our problems to Him. He does not want us to fight while He is handling our case, nor should we worry about how He will act or the methods He will employ. Interfering in the battle can hinder the process and may expose you to severe attacks and injuries from the enemy. God is fully capable of managing every aspect of His responsibilities. He does not require human assistance or approval to resolve a problem. It is always wise to step back and allow the Lord to take charge. However, understand that your absence from the battle does not prevent the enemy from wanting to fight; their conflict is not with you. They will persist in their struggle against the Lord, and no one can confront the Lord and prevail. This is when they will begin to fall into their own traps and be ensnared by their own schemes, as stated in Proverbs 26:27.

Samuel was unsuccessful in his phone call and his brother's trip to Liberia, prompting him to seek alternative means. He filed a complaint with the Georgia State Board of Nursing, alleging that I had been arrested and charged with child abuse and violence against a child in 2019, and that I was currently involved in a rape case investigation. As is standard in any complaint investigation, the board requested evidence to support his claims. Upon receiving this request, Rev. Samuel Siebo and his sibling became overly excited, believing that I would be intimidated by the complaint and would seek to protect my nursing license. They began to celebrate, proclaiming, *"The case will soon be thrown out of court."* They mistakenly thought that my fear of losing my license

Unmasking: A Journey Through Fear to Embrace Reality

would compel me to persuade the child to drop her rape case against her father, who she alleged had molested her for years. Samuel and his siblings were convinced that I had orchestrated the situation and could easily manipulate it. However, they were unaware that I lacked the control they assumed I possessed. He subsequently forwarded the board's response to me through a third party, requesting that I persuade his daughter to take one of three actions:
1. She should fail to appear in court
2. Tell law enforcement that she lied on him about the rape
3. withdraw the case from the court

He urged her to take immediate action. If she failed to do so, he would forward the requested evidence to the nursing board. He set a deadline of May 26, 2023. He received a response from the nursing board on May 15, 2023, and promptly shared that information with me on the same day.

The enemy is aware of the buttons to press to provoke a reaction from you. This is why we must remain vigilant and not grant the enemy access to our decision-making processes or our vulnerabilities. Often, anything that brings you joy can be weaponized against you. Samuel Siebo recognized my weakness; he knew I feared divorce. Consequently, whenever he sought to pursue actions I disapproved of, he would resort to threats that compelled me to retreat. I lived in constant fear throughout my marriage. He became familiar with my apprehension, and thus, he attempted to exploit my past, but this time he encountered a new and resolute version of me. I refused to back down. I awaited the response from the Georgia Board of Nursing regarding his complaint. However, as of this writing, I have yet to receive any communication from the board.

The lesson learned is to never allow the enemy to confront you at the point where they once left you. The devil will invariably use information about you—whether it be sin, your misdeeds, or any secrets you wish to keep hidden—to instill fear and intimidation, compelling you to succumb to his schemes. This is why the Bible cautions us in 1 Peter 5:8 to remain alert and maintain a sound mind, avoiding the clouding of our thoughts with drugs, alcohol, substances, our achievements, wealth, pride, or anything that seeks to control us. When we permit these influences to infiltrate our minds, we lose sight of our true identity in Christ and become ensnared in the enemy's traps. The scripture advises us to remain vigilant against the dangers posed by the enemy, ensuring we do not fall prey to his schemes.

The devil himself lives in constant fear of us, God's children, yet he will never cease his attempts to ensnare us or our children. Unless we remain sober and vigilant, we cannot discern the devil's devices. Samuel Siebo, was asking me to do something that seemed utterly bizarre at that moment. The state and the military had already conducted their investigation; they possessed all the findings and were merely awaiting a hearing date. The wisest course of action for anyone involved in this case was to wait for the hearing. If the accused were found not guilty, or if the court determined the allegations to be false, the case would be dismissed. This was a criminal matter; it was no laughing matter, and he was fully aware of that. However, he had previously taken advantage of my tendency to avoid confrontation, leading him to believe that I would react the same way in this situation. Even if his daughter were to withdraw her case, it would not halt the investigation, as the case had shifted from being between him and his daughter to being between him and the state. She was merely a potential witness for the prosecution. Furthermore, making any rash decision to withdraw the case could potentially jeopardize his daughter's standing with the state. This illustrates that the enemy is indifferent to your well-being; he seeks only to exploit you for his selfish agenda, turning you into a victim. Remember, you are not and cannot be a victim. Resist that notion and that mentality. Do not allow the enemy to witness your tears. Walk with dignity and hold your head high, for you are not the victim; the enemy is the true victim.

CHAPTER 13

The Devilishly Paralyzing Effect of Fear

For Christians, fear can be a powerful adversary, threatening to stifle their faith and paralyze them from living out their beliefs. It can manifest in various forms, from anxieties about health and finances to doubts about God's presence and protection. In its grip, Christians may hesitate to share their faith, engage in challenging situations, or step outside their comfort zones. This fear can lead to spiritual stagnation, hindering growth and hindering the ability to fully embrace God's calling. However, scripture offers solace and guidance, reminding Christians that God does not give us a spirit of fear, but of power, love, and a sound mind. By actively seeking God's strength and relying on His promises, we can overcome fear and move forward in faith, trusting that He will be with them through every challenge. As Christians, we live in a world where people look at the outside appearances and physical attributes of a person and then conclude that it is well with them. But it is only those who know what truly lies beyond the appearances or veils that person wears that can tell the world what the person is going through. As the saying goes, looks can truly be deceiving. Fear and stress can make a person behave abnormally.

After hearing a story about how bishops in the AME Church divorce their wives to marry other women whom they perceive as potential partners to help them ascend to the bishopric, I was taken aback. A part of me felt that Samuel Siebo was sending me a veiled message regarding his intentions toward me. However, being the naïve wife that I was, I dismissed it as mere foolishness. After a few days of reflection, the story began to unsettle me, but understanding the nature of men, I chose to take it with a grain of salt. When Samuel elaborated on the reasons why AME ministers divorce and remarry, my inexperienced mind struggled to accept that the church would permit such actions to occur openly. Consequently, I resisted believing his narrative. I questioned, *"Why would the church allow a lead pastor to abandon his wife without cause and then be elected as a bishop?"*

At that time, I eagerly anticipated witnessing whether the church would truly embody the essence of its teachings and adhere to biblical principles. I hoped to see a church that genuinely cared for the spirituality of its members and supports their growth in all aspects of life. However, I was taken aback by what I encountered. I observed bishops, lead pastors, officers, and members of the AME Church celebrating Samuel for abandoning his family and marrying another woman he met during his campaign for bishop in South Africa. It felt like a profound betrayal. This experience prompted me to reconsider Samuel's claims about divorce and the concept of a marriage of convenience within the AME Church. I began to question whether the former wives of those pastors had been treated similarly to how I was being treated by Samuel

Siebo. My mind was filled with more questions than answers, and my inner turmoil and doubts led me to believe that many of the men of God within the AME Church were more self-serving than devoted to serving God.

Fear can be an incredibly powerful force, gripping us with an icy hand and leaving us paralyzed. It clouds our thoughts, making it challenging to think clearly or devise solutions. In this state of inaction, we find ourselves unable to take the necessary steps to confront the source of our fear. This vulnerability can ensnare us in a cycle of worry and stagnation, hindering our ability to live life to its fullest potential. There have been moments when I could have stood up and done the right thing, actions that could have spared my family and me from numerous headaches and embarrassment. Yet, I hesitated, held back by fear—fear that no one would believe me, fear that others would perceive me as ungrateful for my husband's sacrifices in bringing me and our children to the U.S. and supporting my education. As believers, we are called to act righteously and to represent Christ Jesus here on Earth. However, we often allow our personal feelings and concerns about others' opinions to obstruct God's purpose in our lives.

I believe that a pastor's wife should exemplify grace and quiet strength. Her unwavering faith ought to shine through in her daily interactions, providing comfort and encouragement to those around her. She should serve as a pillar of the church, leading women's groups, organizing events, and consistently extending a warm welcome to newcomers. Simultaneously, she should remain humble, never seeking the spotlight, but instead radiating genuine kindness and warmth. Her life should stand as a testament to the power of faith and service, leaving an indelible mark on the hearts of all who know her.

As the wife of a pastor, I was acutely aware of being observed by others, yet I often found myself distracted by my own inner thoughts. Instead of seeking God's guidance on how to please Him, I became preoccupied with concerns about what others might say about me—particularly regarding my attire in church and whether it met their approval. Many days, I nearly stumbled as I entered the church, fixated on people's facial expressions and their validation. I was afraid to be my true self—the self who could stand among the congregation and worship as if it were just me and God in the room. The self who could kneel in praise and worship, tears streaming down my face, indifferent to who was watching. I strayed from the right path out of fear, living a life of pretense. My efforts to impress those observing me overshadowed my desire to make the Lord proud. As the wife of a pastor, every moment of your life and that of your household is scrutinized. This is why we must strive to be a city on a hill for the Lord. Believe it or not, no matter how hard you try to conceal your true self, people will sense those hidden truths and recognize when you are not being genuine.

I recall receiving a call one Sunday evening after service from a concerned member who asked why my daughter appeared angry during the service. She mentioned, "*I noticed your youngest daughter during the service today; she seemed to be seriously distracted while her father was preaching, and I'm worried if everything is alright with her.*" The truth is, my daughter was grappling with emotions that she couldn't fully understand or articulate. As a result, she internalized her anger and bitterness, which manifested in her behavior, drawing the attention of others.

After our conversation, I reached out to my daughter to share what had been said and to see if she wanted to discuss anything. The moment I posed the question, she broke down in tears, crying uncontrollably. Her siblings and I quickly gathered around her to offer comfort and to understand what she was experiencing.

Eventually, she opened up, saying, "*The church feels deceptive; my father is deceitful. He behaves one way at home and stands in church saying something entirely different, while everyone agrees with him, shouting 'Amen, amen.'*" As a preacher, you are meant to be a beacon of light. Everything associated with you should reflect that light, which is a positive thing if your light serves the purpose of our Lord and Savior, Jesus Christ.

In moments of solitude, I often find myself grappling with numerous questions. For instance, I ponder whether I am the light that God seeks to illuminate His kingdom on earth. Did my actions truly brighten the path for others to follow Christ?

Unmasking: A Journey Through Fear to Embrace Reality

God calls us to be a beacon for His purpose, especially as spiritual leaders (Matthew 5:14-16).
Yet, fear often obstructs our ability to fulfill God's purpose in our lives. I also reflect on whether I have adequately glorified God or if I allowed the fear of losing Samuel Siebo to lead me into deception, and potentially misleading those who trusted me in my role as a pastor's wife. Each time my ex-husband spoke untruths from the pulpit, one or two congregants would approach me afterward, seeking clarification on his statements, particularly when I knew they were blatant lies. This indicated to me that God was testing my trustworthiness and my capacity to influence His servant (my now ex-husband), who had strayed from His will and purpose for ministry. Regrettably, I often responded with agreement, saying, *'Oh yes, that's true,'* thereby perpetuating the falsehoods Reverend Samuel Siebo, was sharing with the congregation. After covering for him in these instances, I would leave feeling disheartened by my own dishonesty. As spouses of ministers, we are called to be helpmates, tasked with nurturing our partners spiritually, morally, mentally, financially, physically, and in every aspect of their lives and ministries. I struggled to confront his lies, prioritizing my own interests as his wife. What I failed to realize was that God was observing my willingness to support His agenda, starting with my own family.

I was only partially committed in my walk with God when it came to safeguarding my marriage. I failed to confront the devil when I noticed his influence manifesting through Samuel, threatening to dismantle my family. Despite my earnest fasting and prayers, I continued to shield and excuse Samuel of his lies and manipulations. I became an unwitting accomplice in deceit, allowing my marriage to become an idol in my life, leading me to act in ways that were not pleasing to God. Marriage is a sacred institution in the eyes of God, and He holds it in high esteem. As the first institution established by God, it carries His blessings for those who honor it. Since God is integral to the covenant of marriage, He will never endorse idolatry.

I often find myself questioning whether God was testing me through the presence of idolaters. My first encounter with idolatry occurred in our village, Gipo, where my father served as the head priest for the idol that the townspeople revered. This idol, known as Gbon, was central to our community's worship. As a child, I observed my father's deep involvement in the rituals surrounding Gbon. As I mentioned in a previous chapter, he was regarded by the men of the village as a god-like figure, second only to Gbon himself. Unfortunately, like my mother, who lacked the power to rescue my father from his idolatrous ways. I found myself in a similar position with my ex-husband, Samuel Siebo; despite my desperate attempts to save our marriage, I was unable to prevent him from lying and ultimately self-destructing. Tragically, our marriage ended in a painful divorce, leaving our children to bear the emotional scars of our struggles.

The devil is indeed real, regardless of whether one chooses to believe it. Often, anything we feel we must possess to attain happiness can be weaponized against us by the devil, our adversary. According to the Old Testament, the Israelites lost their homeland to their enemies and fell into slavery due to their idolatry. They strayed from the teachings they had received, forgetting the God who had delivered them from their troubles, and pursued other deities, much like their ancestors had done in previous generations. The destructive patterns of our parents' households can persistently follow us, leading to our downfall. As children of God, we must remain vigilant against the enemy's schemes. However, we cannot achieve this alone; it requires the grace of God and our complete submission to His will. There are spiritual battles that cannot be won with a half-hearted approach, especially when the devil has established a foothold in our lives, as he did in mine due to my family's history of idolatry. To overcome these challenges, we must consciously avoid all forms of sin.

Throughout our marriage, I remained faithful to Samuel and endeavored to do everything I believed was right for our relationship, even covering up his dishonesty, which was entirely contrary to God's will. Unknowingly, I fortified the devil's foothold in my life, allowing him to 'sift me like wheat.' During this challenging period, God intervened and humbled me by removing the very things that led me astray. Jehovah God is indeed the God of second chances. In biblical times, people faced immediate consequences for dishonesty, yet the Lord spared me and granted me a second chance. The story of Ananias and Sapphira in Acts 5:1-11 serves as a poignant reminder. I can honestly acknowledge that

I played the role of Sapphira in my marriage, lying to protect my ex-husband's reputation.

Regardless of how wicked and sinful your foundation may be, God has the power to deliver you, use you, and elevate you to a place of honor for His glory. A prime example of this is King Hezekiah. Hezekiah emerged from a deeply flawed background; his father, Ahaz, was a malevolent leader. However, Hezekiah did not allow his upbringing to define him. Instead, he remained faithful and committed in his relationship with God. According to 2 Kings Chapter 18, as the king of Judah, Hezekiah dismantled idolatrous images and eliminated places of idol worship. He ruled and lived in accordance with God's commandments, and as a result, God blessed him throughout his reign. Sometimes I ponder, "Is there anyone in the AME churches today willing to emulate King Hezekiah, who chose not to follow the destructive patterns of his father's house? Can we find a Hezekiah in the AME church today, someone who will stand firm for the things of God, thereby enhancing the church's history and their own spiritual journey with God, just as King Hezekiah did?

PART IV
Keep on Moving

CHAPTER 14

It's All in Your Head

During my time as a bedside nurse, I once cared for an 85-year-old patient. From our conversations, it was clear that she had been physically active before her health declined. However, upon her admission to the hospital, she was in such poor condition that she could not sit up unaided. One day, while checking on her during my shift, I overheard the nurse assistant advising her not to get out of bed without calling for help. The assistant handed her the call light, emphasizing the importance of asking for assistance before attempting to rise. In response, the patient confidently declared, *"I may look 85, but I still have the strength I had at 40."* This was a woman who struggled to sit up in bed without support, yet she insisted she could get out on her own. Such a statement likely stemmed from fear—the fear of losing control. Although she was aware of her age, her mind resisted the reality of her physical limitations. The evidence of her age was undeniable; she appeared even older than 85 due to her health issues. Yet, she was reluctant to accept that her strength had diminished beyond her perception. Like many individuals, this 85-year-old woman feared that caregivers would undermine her autonomy.

Fear can serve as a powerful motivator for self-improvement, yet it can also mislead us. When confronted with a decision, a strong emotional reaction such as fear can obscure our judgment. We might

Unmasking: A Journey Through Fear to Embrace Reality

become fixated on potential negative outcomes, exaggerating their significance while neglecting the positive possibilities. This tendency can result in choices driven by the desire to avoid harm rather than the pursuit of opportunities. Ultimately, fear may divert us from the most beneficial course of action, leading us to opt for decisions that feel safe in the moment but may not serve our long-term interests.

How often do we make decisions knowing they may harm us in the long run, yet we proceed out of fear? How frequently do we attempt to escape reality or confront inevitable outcomes? I reflect on my own experience, particularly when my ex-husband, Samuel Siebo, was granted a divorce in my absence, along with everything we had built together during our marriage. When I received the call from my attorney, who had withdrawn from my case, I was overwhelmed with panic. It felt surreal, despite the clear signs of Samuel's deceit and manipulation of both my lawyer and his. Ultimately, my lawyer became his advocate, delivering the devastating news that the divorce had been finalized. Hearing her voice felt like a sharp object piercing my heart; the pain was profound, and I struggled to accept what felt like an immense loss. I was determined to fight for my share of our properties, even after learning that a settlement agreement had been submitted to the court. I refused to believe that my own attorney had sided with my ex-husband—not because I had done anything wrong, but because she sought financial gain from him. At that time, I was financially unable to cover her attorney fees, and she viewed the compromise as an easy way to profit without putting in the effort to fight my case. It was a dark period in my life. I was resolute in my desire to fight, but my struggle felt like that of a toothless bulldog. Sometimes, in life, we must choose our battles wisely and understand how and when to engage in the fight.

It was clear that the attorney was determined not to allow herself to be exposed or shamed by me. She had mishandled my case and was doing everything possible to cover up her mistakes and the conspiracy surrounding it. I felt powerless to fight back due to my financial situation, which she was fully aware of. Samuel Siebo had informed the attorneys that I was inexperienced with the judicial system, leading them to believe I would not challenge the judgment rendered against me. He assured my lawyer that he would pay her fees since I was unable to do so, but in return, she needed to persuade me to transfer all the property we had worked for during our marriage to him. Unfortunately, all our real estate holdings were outside the jurisdiction of the court where our divorce was filed, yet neither Samuel's attorney nor my own informed us of this critical detail. The only property within the court's jurisdiction was our household items, meaning we did not need to divide the real estate during the divorce proceedings.

We could have finalized the divorce and addressed the property division later in the appropriate jurisdictions. Furthermore, Samuel failed to provide any of the financial documents I had requested. His refusal prompted my lawyer to advise me to close the case, claiming it was the best course of action given my inability to continue paying her fees. Whenever I questioned her recommendations, she offered various excuses, insisting that the judge would disapprove of us not dividing the property before going to court. She dismissed all my requests for assistance, stating that Samuel would not agree to any terms she proposed. It felt as though Samuel had the final say in the matter. I was deeply hurt by the deceit and dishonesty displayed by my attorney. At that point, I refused to sign the divorce decree and instructed her to set aside the settlement agreement until I could secure an attorney who would compel Samuel to produce the financial documents I had requested. She declined my request and chose to withdraw from my case. As a result, the divorce proceeded in my absence, leaving me without any representation during the proceedings.

Human beings often prove untrustworthy when it comes to money, as it has the power to alter relationships and motivations. After engaging another attorney to set aside the settlement agreement, she allied herself with Samuel's attorney to oppose both my attorney and me. I am certain of one thing: her actions clearly demonstrated her betrayal. During the divorce proceedings, I disclosed a crucial piece of information to her, which Samuel's attorney later subpoenaed when I filed a motion to set aside the settlement agreement. This information could only have originated from her.

During the discovery phase of the divorce, Samuel requested that I provide details about the $1,200 I used to purchase a piece of land for my mother in Liberia. When she inquired, I explained that I had withdrawn the money in cash from my credit union account with Palmetto Health and deposited it into a third-party account at TD Bank, as per the property owner's request. She mistakenly assumed that I had an account with TD Bank and subsequently advised Samuel to subpoena my bank records there. However, he found no account in my name because I had never opened one.

Moreover, on the Monday we signed the settlement agreement, Samuel finally provided her with a bank statement that I had requested during discovery but which he had previously refused to produce. This statement contained vital information regarding Samuel's spending habits. When I asked her to hand over that document to my attorney, she declined. She was subpoenaed to testify against me during the hearing for my motion to set aside the settlement agreement. Although she compelled me to provide all requested information during discovery, she did not obtain any of Samuel's financial details until after the divorce was finalized.

Before the divorce was finalized, there were clear signs of trouble, yet I chose to endure it all. I repeatedly told myself, *"He's still my husband, regardless of how he treats me; I will remain committed. I have invested too much in this marriage to let it slip away."* This experience of enduring such behavior is prevalent in many African communities and across numerous developing countries. How often have we attempted to be someone we are not out of

Unmasking: A Journey Through Fear to Embrace Reality

fear? How frequently have we tried to fit into a mold that doesn't belong to us? How many times have we lived our lives for the sake of others?

The fear of judgment can be an immense burden, particularly for women in unhealthy relationships. Societal pressures to uphold the appearance of a happy family, coupled with the stigma of perceived *'failure,'* can leave women feeling ensnared. Many women find themselves tormented by the whispers and judgments of friends, family, church members, or even strangers. The anxiety of being labeled a *'weak woman'* who couldn't make her relationship work, along with the dread of gossip and pity, can become a paralyzing force for those experiencing abuse. This fear can stifle a person's voice and hinder them from seeking the support necessary to escape a situation that undermines their well-being. I was once one of those women, trapped by my own fear of what others might say.

I remained in my marriage because, when I reflect on our journey from where we started to where we ended up, letting go felt excruciating. However, did my decision to stay in the marriage benefit me in any way? The answer is a resounding *"NO!"* Remaining in the marriage inflicted more mental trauma on me than any potential gain. I was engaged in an unwinnable struggle against a master manipulator and a deceitful man. This battle caused me more psychological distress than the pain of losing the material possessions I had worked hard for during our time together. Being in an abusive marriage is harmful not only to oneself but also to one's children. After our divorce, my younger daughters turned away from Christianity, and they stopped attending church with me. My youngest daughter now identifies herself as an atheist, influenced by the lies she witnessed her father telling the congregation every Sunday. She expresses disbelief in God, and I believe she remains traumatized by the family turmoil she experienced as a child in what was perceived to be a Christian home. Yet, she still asks me to pray for her whenever she embarks on a new project, despite her claims of atheism. Deep down, she recognizes that there is a supernatural presence that answers prayers. By the end of the divorce, our children came to understand that our lives had been a facade, masked by the pretense of Christianity.

CHAPTER 15

KNOW THE ENEMIES YOU ARE BATTLING

Engaging in a spiritual battle can often feel like grappling with invisible forces. Doubts and temptations frequently cloud your mind, whispering negativity and eroding your resolve. However, within this struggle lies a profound source of strength found in faith. By holding steadfast to your beliefs and aligning yourself with what brings you tranquility, you can resist the encroaching darkness. This battle is not fought with physical might, but rather with unwavering conviction and a spirit that refuses to surrender. Ephesians 6:12 reminds us, *"For we wrestle not against flesh and blood, but against principalities, against powers, against the rulers of the darkness of this world, against spiritual wickedness in high places."* Thus, when you find yourself in conflict, it is crucial to recognize the true enemy you face and the appropriate weapon to wield. Understanding that the weapon for this battle is not of the physical realm, compels you to employ a spiritual weapon to achieve victory.

At the beginning of our divorce, I reached out to Samuel Siebo's mother and one of his younger brothers. They seemed disappointed that Samuel had filed for divorce, especially after he had publicly humiliated me in front of his friends and even expelled my mother from our home. His family assumed that I would walk away from the marriage after such treatment, but I chose to stay. One brother, who appeared sympathetic, praised my character, saying, "*We know you to be a good woman; you're easygoing, shy, and you don't bother anyone. But if Samuel is divorcing you because of your family, he will surely regret it. As far as we know, you did nothing to deserve a divorce.*" After the divorce was finalized, this brother made a Facebook post celebrating their mother's testimony in church about the successful divorce of her son, Samuel Siebo. This did not surprise me, as I was aware that both he and their mother had never liked me. Their disdain for me began when we were still in Africa, after Samuel moved to the United States. It became evident that I was only valued as his wife when he was struggling in Liberia. Once he crossed the Atlantic, and aspired to become a bishop in the AME Church, my worth diminished in their eyes. They were unaware of the struggles we faced, begging my family almost daily for food so we could survive. When I was still in Monrovia, both his brother and mother had cried tears of sorrow upon learning that I had obtained a visa for myself and my children to join my husband in the United States. Years later, I mistakenly thought it would be beneficial to confide in them and seek their support during an unapproved divorce.

Upon reflection, it becomes clear that the divorce was precisely what my ex-husband's mother desired. She never viewed me as a suitable woman from the right tribal group to marry her son. Her wish was for him to distance himself from the family that had supported him during his most challenging times. Whenever she was present, and her son wronged me, she would make peculiar remarks, such as, "*I thought you said you didn't want her; why are you now talking about begging her to stay?*" Despite all that Samuel put me through, I remained steadfast, loving him as a devoted wife should. The thought of leaving him to become a single mother terrified me, especially after raising all our children together. This illustrates the profound impact fear can have on an abused woman; it can compel you to seek refuge in the very place that harms you, rather than escaping from it.

Attributing marital troubles directly to a satanic attack is a complex notion, particularly in a marriage that has faced challenges from the outset due to familial influences. Nevertheless, I believe that certain indicators of a spiritual struggle may manifest in a marriage as an escalating negativity that cannot be accounted for by typical disagreements. This may present as a sudden and persistent rise in distrust, an unusual coldness or hostility, or an obsessive preoccupation with trivial matters that escalate disproportionately. At times, these spirals of negativity felt overwhelming and resisted conventional conflict resolution strategies, especially in my relationship with Samuel. Once I recognized that we could no longer find common ground on even the simplest issues, I immediately understood that these were signs of a spiritual attack.

Reflecting on my marriage to Samuel Siebo, I now recognize that I was under a profound spiritual attack. I was acutely aware that malevolent forces were working against my destiny when Samuel began to express sentiments like, *"No money, no love; you better pick up extra shifts at work to support me and the children."* There was a period when I had little to no family time with my children due to work commitments. During this time, my ex-husband discouraged me from taking a break, as I was the primary breadwinner. He saw me as his ATM machine and disrespected me at the same time. When Samuel started making belittling remarks and hurling insults at me, it became clear that our marriage was vulnerable to external threats.

One particularly painful incident occurred when Samuel allowed another woman to verbally insult me over the phone. When our children confronted him about why he permitted such disrespect, he shifted the blame onto me, claiming I had provoked the woman, who was one of his girlfriends. Aside from the divorce, this was one of the most humiliating moments in my marriage to a man of God who failed to defend me against a woman with whom he was committing adultery. From that moment, I understood that dark forces had seized control of my marriage. My only recourse was to pray for divine intervention and miracles.

During the turmoil in our home, Samuel even threw my elderly mother out of our house. She had been living with us and caring for our children for years. His justification for this cruel act, in the middle of the day and with nowhere for her to go, was my inability to raise $3,500 for his trip to Liberia. His trips were primarily for pleasure rather than for any Christian mission. When questioned about his actions, he callously stated, *"I did it because I knew it would hurt Jennifer and compel her to do what I wanted. I know how much she loves her mother."* I was shocked by the cruelty of the man I had married. It was then that I realized generational curses were at play against me. I also became aware that the enemy was actively working against me when I discovered that my husband was seeking a divorce from Liberia while we were both living in the same house in the United States. All these events unfolded after the 2016 AME Church General Conference. I observed my husband's behavior deteriorate progressively. Although I was aware of the situation, my understanding of how to combat spiritual battles was fundamentally flawed. I found myself waiting and hoping for change without taking the necessary steps to create it.

Sometimes, the only language the enemy understands is violence. You cannot engage in spiritual battles with mere dignity. Scripture clearly states in Matthew 11:12, *"From the days of John the Baptist until now, the kingdom of heaven suffers violence, and only the violent shall take it by force."* Therefore, to win the spiritual warfare I was facing, I had to confront it within the spiritual realm. Winning a spiritual battle is a marathon, not a sprint; it demands constant vigilance. To initiate the battle, you must begin by fortifying your defenses through prayer and meditation, seeking strength and clarity from God. When negativity arises, counter it with the word of God. Additionally, it is beneficial to surround yourself with positive influences and activities that uplift your spirit. In this fight, it is wise to enlist prayer warriors to support you and remember that you are not alone. Seek guidance from religious leaders or trusted mentors, and do not hesitate to reach out for professional help if the darkness feels overwhelming. With perseverance and faith, you can emerge stronger from these inner struggles.

I come from a polygamous family, and I married a man who also had an undercover polygamous background. Samuel Siebo's father was married to multiple women simultaneously in Liberia. According to some prevalent Christian beliefs, our shared family histories made us vulnerable to the enemy's attacks in all our aspirations. To combat these attacks, the victim must recognize and confront the evil forces through prayer and fasting, relying on God to overcome. For a long time, I thought the issues in my marriage stemmed from a foundational curse working against me. Consequently, I engaged in fasting, praying, and seeking deliverance repeatedly, as the curse from my family was evident. My father was a polygamist and an idol worshipper, and although I never directly participated in idol worship or witchcraft practices, I was aware that my family was under a curse due to our bloodline connection. It never crossed my mind that my husband's father was also a polygamist, and with polygamous practices come curses.

Samuel's father was a preacher of the gospel, yet his personal life was marked by contradictions. He was legally married and living with his wife, but he also fathered children with my ex-husband's mother outside of that marriage. It was said that he paid the dowry for this woman when their relationship began. One can only imagine the grief, hurt, and bitterness that must have coursed through his legally married wife, who likely felt compelled to release curses upon him and his lineage for his infidelity. Furthermore, he was simultaneously involved with another woman, leading to a situation where he had multiple partners while still residing with his wife. Family history plays a crucial role in our lives, influencing many aspects of our existence. This is why medical professionals inquire about family history during health assessments, and spirituality is no exception. Unfortunately, many Christians and believers often overlook the significance of this.

  Winning a spiritual battle in your marriage is not about defeating your spouse; rather, it involves overcoming challenges together as a united team in faith. The first step is to recognize the true enemies: negativity, resentment, and a self-centered focus that undermines the marriage. These obstacles can be addressed by turning towards God through prayer and reflection. Enhance your communication by approaching disagreements with empathy and a genuine willingness to listen. Remember the reasons you fell in love, and concentrate on uplifting each other through acts of service and kindness. Be quick to forgive, letting go of past hurts. Lastly, seek common ground in your faith. Engage in reading scriptures together, attending religious services, or simply having open conversations about your spiritual journeys. By collaborating and seeking guidance from the Most High God, you can cultivate

Jennifer Yah Legay

a marriage that stands strong against any spiritual storm.

CHAPTER 16

STOP RUNNING AND FACE YOUR FEAR

Fear is a primal instinct, an innate alarm designed to protect us from harm. However, there are times when this alarm becomes overly sensitive, causing us to flee from situations that may not be as threatening as they seem. We often shy away from making tough decisions, postponing difficult conversations, or allowing our dreams to wither, all because fear whispers doubts in our ears. But what if we chose to confront our fears instead of running from them? In retrospect, I view fear as a teacher rather than a monster. It is an imposter that masquerades as our true selves. Fear can also serve as a signal, indicating that we are pushing our boundaries and striving for something new. By acknowledging our fears, we reclaim our power. We can dismantle fear into manageable steps, such as seeking support from friends or mentors and visualizing our success. Remember, courage is not the absence of fear; it is the act of moving forward despite it. Each time you confront your fear, you chip away at its influence—bit by bit. Conversely, if you let go of your fear, you will experience immense satisfaction and personal growth that comes from stepping outside your comfort zone. You will discover the incredible possibilities that arise when you stop fleeing and start pursuing your dreams. Therefore, as a woman of faith, I encourage you to take a deep breath, acknowledge your fear, and take that first step forward. Always remind yourself, *'You've got this.'*

Although Samuel may have divorced me in absentia, I can firmly place the blame on my lawyer. Our attorneys were supposed to complete several tasks to finalize the process. Specifically, my lawyer was responsible for sending a child support garnishment order to the Kansas Child Support Center and submitting documents to the US Army retirement office so that I could receive a portion of Samuel's military retirement benefits, as we were married throughout his military career until the time of the divorce. Unfortunately, none of these tasks were completed before the divorce was granted.

During this time, Samuel was ordered to pay child support directly to me while the garnishment order was being processed. He reached out to me, and I instructed him to deposit the payments into one of the girls' accounts that we both had access to. He agreed and made payments for a few months. However, for two of those months, he failed to pay the full amount again. His justification was that he had purchased a phone and clothes for Elaine, which led him to deduct those expenses from the child support he was obligated to pay. To avoid confrontation, I reluctantly accepted whatever amount he deposited into the account.

He perceived my passive demeanor and reluctance as a chance to cease child support payments. For a couple of months, he halted the payments, and I chose not to confront him. Once he recognized that he had missed three payments without any inquiry from me, he started boasting to his friends, *"I'm* not going to give her another penny for child support. In fact, I will ensure that we split custody of the girls so that I can avoid paying child support altogether."

He refused to pay child support for about eight months. During that time, he continued to treat me as his wife and used our children to benefit from military assistance. When the U.S. Government issued $1,400 during the COVID-19 pandemic, Samuel received a total of $9,800, in addition to two other pandemic payments deposited into his bank account. The government allocated this money to our family based on the number of individuals listed on our tax return from the previous year. Although he informed me about the funds, he refused to share any of it with me or the girls.

When he underwent a Permanent Change of Station (PCS) from Fort Riley to Fort Bragg, the military compensated him for relocating me and the girls, yet he still neglected to pay child support. Instead, he utilized the pandemic and military relocation funds to invest in a home in North Carolina. He then began using that very house to persuade the children to distance themselves from me and come to live with him. He would tell them, *"Why would you want to stay in that cramped apartment when I have a mansion here with a theater? Come live with me; you will each have your own bedroom, and I will buy you a car when you turn 16."*

Despite his refusal to pay child support, I chose not to confront him. I decided to care for my children with the resources I had. I simply did not want to endure the court process again to pursue child support. For me, the court experience was exhausting, particularly due to the fabrications Samuel Siebo consistently presented to the court.

We had shared custody of Elaine and JoAnn, so when it was time for him to have the children, I allowed them to go without any issues. They spent the 2020 winter break with him. During that time, he took the opportunity to poison their minds against me, hoping to keep them in North Carolina. He disregarded the fact that the children were in school. While Elaine refused to stay, he succeeded in keeping JoAnn. He kept JoAnn out of school for an entire week, prompting the school to call several times to inquire about her absence. In the meantime, he lied to the school, claiming that JoAnn had moved to North Carolina.

The school repeatedly contacted me to determine JoAnn's whereabouts, as I was her primary parent residing in the school district. Meanwhile, JoAnn kept calling and pleading with me to come and get her from North Carolina. Initially, she thought it was fun to stay with her father, unaware that his decision would result in her missing school. Our daughter is passionate about her education; no one jokes around when it comes to JoAnn's schooling. As a child, you could take anything away from her, but you could never stop her from attending school. I reached out to my attorney to explain the situation. He instructed Samuel's lawyer to tell him to return JoAnn to Ohio. When that failed, my attorney filed a motion for contempt of court. Despite the contempt order, Samuel refused to return JoAnn. After several unsuccessful attempts to persuade him, I took Elaine and we drove 18 hours round trip from Ohio to North Carolina to retrieve JoAnn. As a result, Samuel was charged with contempt of court.

The court's decision to charge Samuel with contempt only exacerbated the situation for the girls and me. He began to frequently engage in FaceTime videos with JoAnn, showcasing every new item he acquired for his home. *"Look, I just added chairs to the theater! Check out your bedroom; isn't your bedroom set beautiful?"* he would exclaim. Caught up in his web of affluence, he even boasted to the court about his four-bedroom house, complete with a theater and a swimming pool, claiming that the girls could each have their own room instead of sharing one. He would call JoAnn and say, *"You know, when she forces you to stay over there, it could lead to you and Elaine fighting, and if you hurt each other, that might jeopardize her custody of both of you."* Rev. Samuel Siebo began to subtly incite discord between JoAnn and her sister. One day, while I was at work, the two girls got into a physical altercation. Samuel, despite being in North Carolina, was the first to inform me about the fight. He texted me the details, seemingly as a way to build his case for the court. His relentless pursuit to hurt my feelings overshadowed any concern for the safety and well-being of the children. This sheer malice terrified me to my core.

He sought to modify the parenting plan in Kansas

during the contempt hearing, but the court was unable to proceed since we were all outside of Kansas. Both of us needed to agree to the modification in Kansas, but I was reluctant to do so because I believed that Samuel had undue influence over the court in that region. Instead, he filed for modification in Ohio, where the girls and I were currently residing. He then began to tell JoAnn, "*You can inform the judge that you don't want to live with her. You have more opportunities where I live. In Ohio, children can express to the court which parent they prefer to be with.*" While his motion for modification was still pending, he called me to request that I drop the child support order against him. He promised, "*If you drop the child support, I will allow both girls to stay with you. They won't even need to visit me anymore.*" I firmly refused his demand and hired an attorney to represent me in the Ohio case. Although he initiated the modification process, it ultimately did not succeed. Subsequently, we learned that Samuel's attorney had withdrawn from his case. I am uncertain about the details, but I believe that prayer has its power. My Ohio attorney refunded all the fees I had paid, including the guardian ad litem costs. Following this incident, Samuel chose to stop paying child support altogether, and he was furious, like a devil in hell.

As previously mentioned, my relocation to Ohio was not a planned decision; rather, I viewed it as a better choice at the time. My cousin had offered me a place to stay, which was crucial since I had no work history for the past year, despite being a Registered Nurse by profession. This move served as a starting point for me to rebuild my life after my divorce. Although I didn't have a specific state in mind where I wanted to live, I was determined to find a job that would allow me to buy a home for myself and my daughters.

While in Ohio, I applied for jobs at multiple places, one of which was Emory Healthcare in Atlanta, Georgia. Before the termination of the parenting plan modification case in Ohio, I received a job offer from Emory Healthcare. Upon receiving this offer, I informed my landlord that I would not be renewing my rental lease, which was set to expire in May 2021. I also notified my lawyer about my move to Georgia to start my new job. Consequently, I opted for a month-to-month rental arrangement as I prepared to relocate.

I moved to Georgia on June 11, 2021, and began working on June 14, 2021, while my daughters, Elaine and JoAnn, were still with their father for his summer parenting term. Before my move, I reached out to Dr. Somo Hubbard Barsir to inform her of my plans and seek her advice, as she lived and worked in Georgia. Somo is my cousin through my foster family connections, and I had met her for the first time in July 2017 during my ex-husband's younger brother's wedding, where my brother-in-law was marrying Somo's cousin.

During our conversation about my move, Somo graciously offered me a place to stay with her and her family until I could secure my own home, rather than renting a place. Being with Somo and her family felt like a long-standing connection, and I truly believe that my time with them was a divine blessing. They played a significant role in my transition to Georgia.

I lived with Somo and her family from June 11, 2021, to August 7, 2021. On August 8, 2021, I brought Elaine and JoAnn from South Carolina, and we temporarily moved into an Airbnb and then an Extended Stay hotel. We stayed there while I worked until I was able to purchase and move into my new home. Up to this point, Samuel was still refusing to pay for child support.

After almost eight months of him not paying child support, I received an email from my attorney in Kansas asking me whether the girls and I were okay. He asked me about the modification case in Ohio. I told him that Samuel's attorney withdrew from his case and that Samuel had not paid child support for almost eight months. His response was, *"Well then put in the garnishment paperwork that should have been done during the time of the divorce. With that in place you don't have to run after him for child support."* "Sir, I don't want to go through this again," I replied. He then sent me a response with a little more detail about the process, *"You don't have to go through anything,"* he said. *"Pay me and I will do everything for you. I will do the paperwork and send it to the Kansas child support center and to the military financial office, you don't have to appear in court."* I was a bit hesitant to give him the go ahead, but I later agreed to let him handle it since I would not have to go to court. When Samuel found out that a garnishment order was being prepared, he sent me the following text message, *"Jennifer, kindly give me a call. I want to have a conversation with you."* I did not respond to his text because I knew that it was about the garnishment paperwork. Prior to that filing, he didn't talk to me or the children. At that point I was not ready to have any form of conversation with him, especially if it had to do with the garnishment. My attorney did the paperwork and submitted it. When I did not call him I receive this text message from him,

> *"I can't believe you would do this to me; take me to court to garnish my income, after I have done everything I did for you! From January 1st to December 31st, 2021, I spent $37,000.00 on you ($8,000.00 to Ms. Alt, little over $20,000.00 Parent plus loan paid off your credit and $9,000.00 child support-January to June). I tried talking to you about child support payment, but you refused to listen. I had to quit paying you in order to make financial adjustments for myself. You decided to take me to court to force money out of me, without any consideration of what I spent on you in a very short period of time. For five years I supported you in Africa to the very best of my ability. For additional 10 years, I got you to this country, educated you and fully supported you to the professional level where you are. You decided to take advantage of me, after I had invested*

so much in you. Can you see how evil you are? I painfully regret the day I got to know you and I curse the day I approached you about the relationship. I wish I had never known you in my lifetime and I wish I could unknown you even right now! You believe you have gotten away with murder but except there is no God in Heaven, that's the only way you will not receive the wrath of God as revenge for robbing this man of God (me), of every investment I made in you. Go ahead, enjoy my sweat today, you will see what tomorrow will bring!"

Upon receiving the text message from Samuel, I found myself reflecting, *"Is this how those who mistreat others respond when confronted with reality?"* I was indifferent to the falsehoods he shared regarding his supposed contributions to my life, which he relayed to his friends and audience. I had grown accustomed to hearing Rev. Samuel Siebo spread malicious lies about me. When someone tells lies repeatedly, they become desensitized to the truth and start to believe their own fabrications. Samuel has become adept at disseminating such disinformation about me, so it was not something I felt compelled to dwell on or worry about.

What perplexes me about his message is that he identifies himself as a man of God, yet claims that God will avenge his grievances against me for compelling him to support his children. Not only does he seek divine retribution for fulfilling his familial responsibilities, but he also equates his obligation to support his children with being victimized. In my view, there is no room for complacency when confronting evil. Those who inflict harm, manipulate, or exploit others choose a path that undermines the very fabric of a just and compassionate society. While forgiveness and understanding can be important, genuine support must be built on a foundation of decency. Samuel Siebo, is neither decent nor moral. As children of God, we must not condone cruelty, nor should we remain silent while others suffer. It is through actively opposing negativity, fostering empathy, and holding wrongdoers accountable that we can cultivate a society where goodness thrives and evil ultimately collapses under its own weight.

1 Timothy 5:8 plainly tells us, *"But if any provide not for his own, and especially for those of his house, he hath denied the faith, and is worse than an infidel."* The enemy, often referred to as the devil, is incredibly cunning. He will look you in the eye and deceive you with lies, aiming to lead you into poor decisions or to make you give up. Stand firm against him, and he will retreat from you, as stated in James 4:7. People may employ fear as a tactic to dishearten you, to undermine your spirit, or to instill disappointment, pushing you to abandon your aspirations. You are not obligated to accept their falsehoods. I spent a significant part of my life in fear alongside Reverend Samuel Siebo. The issues he raised in his text message were among the many factors that kept me living in that state of fear.

Whenever he would say to me, *"I brought you to America."* Then I began to feel guilty and not even think of myself as the avenue which God used to bring Samuel to America. I became a slave to fear. In the book titled 'Leviathan Exposed Overcoming the Hidden Schemes of a Demonic King', Robert Hotchkin said, *"Fear works like faith, only in a negative way. Fear is a landing strip for the enemy. It draws him, gives him a place, and empowers him."* Therefore, you must fight against the enemy and wicked spirits or powers that are working in them to destroy you. You can't continue to run from the enemy forever. Fight back standing on the word of God and the blood of Jesus. Robert Hotchkin further tells us *"we don't become great champions by avoiding battles, but rather by embracing them and allowing the Lord to teach us how to lay hold of victory in every situation we face."*

The story about the four lepers in 2 Kings chapter 7 is a clear indication of why we should face our battles and not run from it. This story is told of four lepers that were thrown outside the gate of their city because they were considered to be contiguous due to leprosy. They weren't thrown out under normal circumstances where they could get help from family or friends. But they were ostracized when there was severe famine in their land. It is told in 6 Chapter of 2 Kings that there was severe hunger in their land during this time until women began to eat their babies. But *"Man's extremity is God's opportunity of making his own power to be glorious. His time to appear for His people is when their strength *is gone."* Matthew Henry's commentary on 2 Kings 7:1-2." This is true when we yell to the voice of God and follow His lead. Notice that the four lepers were considered outcasts, and they were put outside the city to die due to their disease conditions. Imagine them sitting there without hope. That's what the enemy wants you to do in your fear. To sit and worry, have self-pity, to get caught up in bitterness and miss your blessings. The four lepers refused to be hindered by fear, they refused to listen to the voice of the enemy. They acknowledged their fear, and they moved toward it. They recognized their reality of being in imminent danger, and they decided we would face it anyway. They said to themselves we will face our fears and whatever the outcome is, we will accept because not facing it puts us in equal harm as facing it.

"And they said one to another, why sit here until we die? If we say, we will enter into the city, then the famine is in the city, and we shall die there. And if we sit still here, we die also, now therefore come, and let us fall unto the host of the Syrians. If they save us alive, we shall live; and if they kill us, we shall but die." 2 Kings 7:3-4. The four lepers got up and went and they saved their nation from hunger. Through them prophecies were fulfilled. Be willing to move on and try every possible way to alleviate your fear. You may not have physical condition like the four lepers. Sometimes, your Leprosy could be family members tormenting your marriage. It could be an unfaithful husband, envious family members, or friends. It could be your generational background preventing you from achieving your goals in life.

Jennifer Yah Legay

Overcoming your fears requires immense courage and motivation. When you confront your fears, you may face criticism from others; friends might distance themselves, and family members may turn their backs and hurl insults. In such moments, will you choose to remain in the shadows, consumed by grief? Or will you rise, like the four lepers, and embrace life? Reflect on your identity, your purpose, and your current circumstances. Your struggles may be the very means through which the Lord intends to bring deliverance to your family, community, or even your nation, just as He did with the four lepers. They chose to rise and take action, exposing themselves to the world, and through their bravery, prophecies were fulfilled.

PART V
THROUGH IT ALL, I WON!

CHAPTER 17

LIFE IN SOUTH CAROLINA

South Carolina has a mystique to it. The state beckons with its allure of Southern charm, beautiful beaches, and a slower pace of life for many of its native sons and daughters. But beyond the postcard image, there's a lot to consider for those contemplating a move. If you crave sunshine, South Carolina delivers. With mild winters and long summers, outdoor enthusiasts will find plenty to explore, from kayaking through cypress swamps to golfing on world-class courses. The vibrant coastal towns like Charleston and Myrtle Beach offer a taste of history alongside fresh seafood and buzzing nightlife. Beyond the coast, charming cities like Greenville boast a thriving arts scene and a growing culinary reputation. Lexington County which is suburb to Columbia is situated right by the manmade Lake Murray which is to the north side of the Town of Lexington. Lake Murray is known for its countless boating, kayaking, and its beautiful views when driving by the lake.

The lifestyle in South Carolina may not suit everyone. I discovered this firsthand when I relocated there with my family. The hot and humid summers can be quite a shock for those accustomed to cooler climates. Although the cost of living is generally lower than the national average, housing prices in popular areas are steadily increasing. Public transportation options are limited, particularly outside major cities, making a car essential for getting around. Furthermore, while the state is known for its friendly atmosphere, it is crucial to show respect for the local culture and way of life. My upbringing in Liberia helped me integrate smoothly into this new environment.

Ultimately, the choice to relocate to South Carolina hinged on our priorities at that moment. If you seek a connection to nature, a more relaxed lifestyle, and a genuine taste of Southern hospitality, South Carolina may be the ideal place for you. I always advise individuals to conduct thorough research by visiting various regions to truly experience the atmosphere and carefully consider the advantages and disadvantages before making such a significant move.

On the other hand, Johnson City, Tennessee, was a wonderful place for families. We were fortunate to be surrounded by incredible people who significantly impacted our lives. However, after Samuel faced multiple job terminations in the Johnson City area, he concluded that it was no longer a suitable place for us to live, especially after his dismissal from Core Services. This prompted him to consider relocation options. He believed that South Carolina would be the ideal destination, as it felt like his second home in the U.S.

Samuel later informed me about a hospital chaplain training position in Columbia, South Carolina, which he had applied for and was called in for an interview. In mid-July 2011, our family made a quick trip to South Carolina for Samuel's interview.

During that trip, I contacted the human resources office at Palmetto Health to inquire about registered nurse positions for new graduates. The representative I spoke with asked for some time to check and promised to call me back.

Within an hour, she called back with good news: she had multiple interview appointments available for me the following day, should I be interested. This was the same hospital system where Samuel was interviewing, and I was eager to pursue a job there. Without hesitation, I attended the interview on July 14, 2011, and received a job offer on the spot. Samuel was also accepted into the hospital chaplaincy training program, which was a paid training lasting nine months. From that moment on, we were both confident about our jobs in South Carolina and decided to search for a home there.

Our goal was to move into our own home upon relocating, rather than renting an apartment. Samuel reached out to a realtor in South Carolina, and we made several trips to view potential homes. After I accepted the job offer, the hiring manager wanted me to start on July 25, 2011. However, I was concerned about my employment at Johnson City Medical Center, where I had not worked for nearly two months. In a conversation with Samuel, I expressed my worry about how to inform my manager of my departure on such short notice. Samuel reassured me, saying, *"Don't you want your own home? You're worried about those hospitals that profit at the expense of their employees? We've already put down earnest money on the home, and if we miss the deadline, we could lose it.*" His words struck fear in me; I didn't want to forfeit my $1,500 earnest money to a developer. Consequently, I decided to give my employer in Johnson City one week's notice.

Despite this, I still could not start work in South Carolina on July 25, 2011, as we were focused on securing a home before our move, necessitating multiple trips back and forth to South Carolina. I informed the hiring manager that I could not begin on the original date, and my new start date was set for August 8, 2011. During that time, we found a home we liked, but when we met with the banker or underwriter, we learned that we could not secure the loan because we needed to have worked in the state and provide at least three months of pay stubs to qualify.

Upon hearing the news, we decided to search for a rental home. We discovered a charming 3-bedroom, one-level house in a family-friendly subdivision right next to Lexington High School in Lexington, South Carolina. That weekend, we were all in South Carolina looking for the perfect rental, and we completed the paperwork for the home on August 5, 2011. On Monday, August 8, 2011, after my initial orientation at work, we received the keys to our new home. I stayed in South Carolina for work and moved in using an air mattress, while Samuel and our daughters returned to Johnson City to pack our belongings for the move. They later came back to South Carolina to pick me up, allowing me to drive our family Chrysler Pacifica with the girls during the relocation, while Samuel drove the U-Haul truck filled with our household items.

We officially moved to South Carolina on August 14, 2011, arriving at our new rental home around 8:00 PM Eastern Time. Samuel, having lived and attended school in South Carolina, was familiar with many members of the Liberian community there. He informed some of his friends about our relocation, and a few came to help us unload the U-Haul truck. As is often the case with moving, we faced challenges in finding our way and making new friends. However, thanks to the welcoming Liberian community in the Columbia area, these challenges were minimal. We quickly adapted to our new surroundings.

Lexington County boasted one of the finest school systems in South Carolina, with their District School consistently ranked as the best in the state. This reputation was a significant factor in my decision to relocate to Lexington. We were able to swiftly enroll our daughters in their respective schools: Elaine began her journey at Rocky Creek Elementary School in first grade, Louise attended Pleasant Hill Middle School in the eighth grade, and Ernestine started at Lexington High School in the ninth grade. At that time, JoAnn was just four years old and would cry every morning as she watched Elaine board the school bus, yearning to join her sister in the adventure of school. Unfortunately, she was not accepted into the pre-kindergarten program at Rocky Creek, which made me nostalgic for Johnson City, Tennessee. In Johnson City, we lived conveniently close to the Head Start Daycare, where

Unmasking: A Journey Through Fear to Embrace Reality

JoAnn had been welcomed into the program before our move. Regrettably, the Head Start in Lexington was not accepting new students, leaving JoAnn to be at home.

There were occasions when our four-year-old had to stay alone in the house until I returned from work. Samuel worked during the day and left early in the morning, while I worked nights, aiming to arrive home before Ernestine left for school. I would drop Ernestine off at her school, which was just a stone's throw away from our home, as her classes did not start early. However, there were times when I couldn't leave work early enough to ensure I was home in time for her. Consequently, we had to leave JoAnn alone in the house. Reflecting on that period, I feel a pang of guilt for putting my baby girl in such a risky situation. One positive aspect was that JoAnn was an exceptionally good listener; she followed our instructions meticulously. We had told her not to open the door for anyone and to remain in her room until I returned home in the morning. True to her word, JoAnn stayed in her room, even ignoring my calls when I entered the house. I would have to go to her room, and only when she physically saw me would she come out. We were acutely aware of the risks involved, but at that point, we felt we had no other choice. After some time at my new job and with a few overtime hours, we finally managed to enroll JoAnn in the daycare pre-K program, and she absolutely loved her new school.

Although it was disappointing not to relocate to a home of our own in South Carolina, I remained undeterred in my pursuit of our goal. Instead, I was motivated to take on extra shifts to meet the income requirements for our future home while Samuel and the girls searched for properties. My income was crucial for securing the loan, as Samuel's nine months of chaplaincy training at the hospital was not deemed a reliable source of income by the bank for a mortgage. After six months of diligent work, we returned to the bank, where the loan agent informed us that I exceeded the income requirements for an FHA loan. However, we ultimately qualified for a conventional loan. Meanwhile, Samuel and our daughters discovered a beautiful all-brick, five-bedroom home that was still under construction. After securing the loan, we successfully closed on the home on May 4, 2012.

Owning a new home was an exhilarating experience. I worked extra hours to save money for furnishing our new space. On the day we closed on the house, I made a quick stop at the office to sign the closing documents before heading to work. Samuel and one of his younger brothers, whom we had just brought to the USA, accompanied us to the signing. I was unaware of the protocols involved in signing mortgage or home ownership documents, and it was during our home closing in 2012 that I learned about them. Samuel and his brother arrived ahead of me, and when I got there, they were already seated. The attorney, or whoever was in charge, instructed Samuel to get up because he was occupying my seat. I explained that Samuel is my husband, but the attorney replied, *"I know, but he's the cosigner, so let him sit further down."* The situation was embarrassing, especially considering Samuel's pride; he didn't want it to be known that my income was the basis for our loan. I asked the attorney, *"Can I waive that right to my husband and let him remain in his seat?"* He responded, *"Yes, but we will have to pass the documents to you, and you can sign them and pass them on to him, as that's how we have arranged it."*

Throughout our marriage, I waived many rights to Samuel, but it seemed to mean little to him. Regardless, we moved into our home, and we were all thrilled to have a place to call our own. Shortly after settling in, Samuel's chaplaincy training with the hospital concluded, leaving him unemployed for a while. However, he was accepted into US Army basic combat training in mid-2012, which was a paid position for three months. He received his orders for training, and we needed someone to stay home with our daughters while he was away, especially to help Elaine and JoAnn with the school bus. One day, while we were sitting at the dining table, Samuel announced, *"I'm going to bring my mother to take care of the children."* I replied, *"Doty boy, don't you think it would be embarrassing to leave my mother, who has been caring for the children, and bring your mother in instead? The kids aren't used to being with her."* He became upset with my comment and retorted, *"Well, I will bring my mother. If you don't like it, you can leave, but I'm bringing her!"* After his outburst, he got up from the table and walked away. I sat in silence for a long time before going upstairs.

Two weeks later, he returned home excited and said, "I want us to bargain." I was confused and asked, *"Bargain on what?"* He proposed, *"How about I bring your mother, and then I bring my mother?"* I was lying on my stomach, but I turned around and asked, *"Who's the friend you spoke with today? Do you think I don't have my head on my shoulders?"* He replied, *"I know you do, but that statement isn't directly from you."* I suspected he had spoken with a friend who advised him to bring both mothers to avoid tension between us, as my mother had been the primary caregiver for our children.

Truth be told, throughout our marriage, I never directly benefited from anything Samuel did without having to give or do something in return. To summarize, after discussing the idea of him bringing both mothers, he requested that I raise funds for him to bring my mother over. I took on extra shifts and successfully raised the money he needed. Subsequently, he wrote an invitation letter using his military orders to request a visiting visa from the embassy for my mother, so she could come and help care for our children while he underwent basic combat training. He went to the embassy with my mother, and presented the letter and she was granted a visa. She arrived in the United States in September 2012. Upon her arrival, we instructed her not to answer calls that weren't directed to her and to hang up when we were on the phone. My mother followed these guidelines without issue, and our only challenge was teaching her how to use the utensils in our home.

Unmasking: A Journey Through Fear to Embrace Reality

When Samuel was about to graduate from his military combat training school in December 2012, he wrote another invitation letter for his mother. She obtained her U.S. Visa and arrived in December 2012. Upon her arrival at our home, she disregarded all the rules we had established and acted contrary to our requests. Samuel apologized numerous times during her brief stay with us. She seemed to believe that everything in our home belonged to Samuel, which led her to feel that she did not need to consult me about anything. Furthermore, she did not perceive her visit to America as an opportunity to care for our children without compensation. She boldly declared, *"I'm not going to take care of anybody's children if they don't pay me."*

After Samuel graduated from Basic Combat Training in December 2012, he found himself without a salary for a while as he awaited selection for a regular army unit. He felt embarrassed to stay home all day and was determined to keep his mother unaware of his unemployment. Consequently, he would leave the house for a while and return only when he felt comfortable. Meanwhile, I continued to work while he managed the household. He took the children out, and our family managed to cope. In May 2013, he was selected for a regular army unit and was sent to El Paso, Texas, in preparation for deployment to Afghanistan, while the girls and I remained in South Carolina with the mothers. Samuel was deployed to Afghanistan from January 1, 2014, to September 14, 2014. A few months after his return from deployment, he was assigned to Fort Jackson, South Carolina, in 2015. This marked the moment when we were all reunited as a family once again.

When Samuel got the army chaplaincy job, I decided to go back to school for my Master of Science in Nursing, since we now had two family incomes. I started school in August 2013 and when he was assigned to El Paso, Taxes, I was now the only driver in the house. I had to take care of the children while I worked and went to school full-time. To have some flexibility at work, I decided to join the float pool in an as needed position. Although I worked in this position, my pay rate was higher, and there were times when I made more money than when I worked the full-time position. Also, Samuel had a steady income from the military, and we were better off financially. Initially when I started school Samuel didn't have a problem with me going to school because my income got better instead, since the hourly rate was higher than previous pay.

 As I progressed through the program and began my clinical classes, I found it challenging to work as many hours as I had in the past. This change did not sit well with Samuel, who was unhappy about the decrease in my income. He expected me to bring home the same paycheck I had when he was not working. One Saturday morning, after returning from work, I reminded him about the funeral of one of his friend's mother-in-law. I encouraged him to attend to show support for his friend's family. After returning from the funeral, I changed into comfortable clothes and went to sleep, having worked the previous Friday night without any rest before the funeral. Since I had already worked overtime during that pay period, I felt justified in prioritizing my sleep.

When I informed Samuel that I would not be working that night, he became furious. He was unwilling to accept my decision, stating, *"You know that overtime is what brings in more money, and I didn't realize that attending the funeral would prevent you from working. Had I known, I wouldn't have gone with you to the funeral."* I felt disappointed by his reaction but chose to brush it off. A week later, he confronted me, saying, *"I see that your income has decreased, so I want us to split the bills."* I replied, *"How can I split the bills with you when I'm in school and taking clinical classes?"* He responded, *"Your income has dropped, and I can't continue to cover the majority of the bills."* Of course, my income had decreased because I was no longer working extra hours. However, it had not dropped to a level that necessitated Samuel covering most of our expenses.

In mid-2015, he insisted on splitting the bills, so I agreed to take on the mortgage, viewing it as a single significant bill rather than multiple smaller ones that I might forget to pay. Ultimately, I discovered that I didn't need to worry about missing payments because Samuel was still responsible for writing the checks for all our bills. In hindsight, I realized this was another form of manipulation; despite his insistence on splitting the bills, he maintained control over our finances. He managed our accounts, transferring money as he pleased and making decisions without my input.

I continued to work and had sufficient funds in my account to cover the mortgage, even while attending school. Although I missed a couple of paychecks due to traveling out of state for clinicals, I managed to work during my school breaks to recover those lost earnings. I felt disappointed when he asked me to split the bills, but I remained patient and supportive throughout my time in school. During his campaign to become bishop in 2016, I took on extra shifts to help raise funds for the campaign. The AMEC conference to elect bishops took place in Philadelphia from July 6 to July 13, 2016, but unfortunately, Samuel was not elected. By the end of the conference, we were all exhausted from sleepless hours of campaigning, yet we had to drive back to South Carolina for 12 hours. Samuel, Louise, and I drove back in the three vehicles we had taken to Philadelphia. Due to our fatigue from lack of sleep and extensive walking during the campaign, we couldn't complete the 12-hour drive home in one go. Therefore, we decided to stop somewhere between Virginia and North Carolina to rest for the night. The next morning, we resumed our journey for the final stretch to South Carolina. We arrived in South Carolina by late afternoon and quickly returned to our routine of work and school, reuniting as a family.

Samuel mentioned that his mother frequently pressured him for money, prompting him to find her a job in New Jersey after our return from Philadelphia. She secured a position with a woman who needed someone to care for her child while she was at work. Unbeknownst to me, Samuel and his mother were also planning a vacation to Liberia in March 2017. I only learned of this when he asked me to work extra shifts to raise $3,500 for his spending money for the trip. I explained that it was impossible for me to gather that amount, as I was busy completing my graduate program and preparing for my board certification exam. Consequently, I offered to assist with whatever I could. I graduated from my MSN program in December 2016 and managed to work a few shifts, raising $1,500 for his pocket money for Liberia. Unfortunately, this did not sit well with him, and he was quite upset.

I sat for my NP national certification board exam in February 2017 and successfully passed. Prior to that, I had a job offer waiting for me, contingent upon my passing the board. However, I didn't begin my new role until May 2017 due to the hospital credentialing process. In March 2017, Samuel and his mother traveled to Liberia, and he returned in April 2017, filled with anger and resentment. I understood that his frustration stemmed from my inability to raise the amount of money he had requested. At that time, I had a plan I wanted to discuss with him, and I refused to let his attitude intimidate me. I told him we needed to talk, and he agreed.

One evening, while we were in our bedroom, I explained that once I started my new role as a nurse practitioner, I would be removing him from my account, and I provided my reasons. I had worked hard and contributed to everything Samuel wanted for himself and his family, yet not once did he acknowledge Jennifer's role in these contributions. I felt unrecognized by him and his family for my efforts. Additionally, he insisted that we split our bill payments, despite having a steady job and managing our finances. His response to my concerns was, *"You are not woman enough to take me off your account."* Nevertheless, I did remove him from my account. However, my contributions to our shared responsibilities in the house remained unchanged. The only difference was that he no longer had direct access to my account, which drove him to the brink of frustration. He remarked, *"No money, no love."*

The turmoil in our home and marriage escalated dramatically. Throughout our relationship, we experienced misunderstandings and arguments, but for Samuel, removing him from my account signified the end of our marriage—he seemed to desire my money more than me. He was unwilling to change his behavior; all he wanted was to be reinstated on my account. His arrogance grew, and he became verbally abusive, showing no regard for the hurtful things he said about me to others. Samuel spread malicious rumors, calling me derogatory names and referring to me as an 'old dirty woman,' questioning why he ever married me in the first place. He openly discussed our intimate life with anyone who would listen, lamenting his lack of enjoyment and expressing regret over our marriage. This behavior extended to his friends and younger siblings, many of whom reached out to me to share the hurtful things he had said. The shame and humiliation I felt upon hearing these stories were overwhelming.

Unmasking: A Journey Through Fear to Embrace Reality

Samuel even went so far as to discuss the female genital mutilation (FGM) I underwent as a child in our village, Gipo, with our children. I had assumed that Ernestine and Louise were aware of this, as it was part of our immigration story to the United States, but I believed they had forgotten due to their young age at the time. The first to inquire about it was Ernestine. One Saturday morning, after a driving lesson with Samuel, she approached me in the kitchen and asked, 'Mamie, daddy said they did something to your private part, what is that?' At that moment, I felt utterly exposed, as if something inside me had died. My only response was a shocked, 'What!?' She clarified, 'Yes, but I didn't understand what daddy was talking about.'

A week later, on a Sunday afternoon, Louise called to tell me, 'Mamie, your husband called me and wanted to speak poorly about you on the phone. I told him I wouldn't allow him to talk about my mother like that. If there's an issue, we need to sit down and discuss it. I'm coming over for a family talk, and I've informed Ernestine.' However, that family conversation did little to alleviate the shame and humiliation I felt from Samuel's discussions about me with his friends, siblings, and even our children. His behavior became increasingly unacceptable, and our home turned into a place of misery. I often found myself contemplating suicide, feeling that I had to endure for the sake of my children. Each time I entered my car in the parking garage, tears would flow. I confided in Samuel about my suicidal thoughts, but he mocked me, sending a long email that suggested he would be exempt from blame if something were to happen to me.

I often dreaded returning home, as the atmosphere was tense without Samuel having access to my account. He was loud and angry, and conversations became impossible. He began leaving the house for days without informing us of his whereabouts, ignoring our calls. On several occasions, I had to contact the police to report his absence. Despite all this, I remained resolute in my decision to keep him off my account, determined to see some acknowledgment or change from him. Instead, he resisted my decision even more fiercely.

In June 2017, he entered my mother's room one afternoon, took all her belongings, and threw them out onto our driveway. He then told her to leave the house. I had worked the night before and was preparing to return to work that evening, so I was asleep when he discarded her things. After placing her belongings outside, he woke me up and said, "*I put your mother's things outside. Find a place for her before you go to work because she can't stay in this house tonight.*" Hearing this, I jumped up and rushed to get my mother, concerned for her health due to her high blood pressure condition. When I reached her, she was standing in the kitchen, visibly shaky and nervous. I urged her to sit down and checked her blood pressure, which was mildly elevated. I promptly gave her medication and sat with her to provide comfort. I then called a friend of mine and explained the situation. Without hesitation, she offered to take my mother in until I could sort things out. My mother stayed in my friend and her husband's home for couple of months, until I was able to take her back to Liberia.

The following day, Samuel called again and began disparaging me to people we knew, including family members. He recounted how he had thrown my mother out of our home. One of my sisters misunderstood his words, thinking he meant he would throw her out. She pleaded with him not to put his mother-in-law outside. Her appeal seemed to inflate his ego further. He became boastful about his actions, believing there was nothing anyone could do to stop him. He didn't stop there; he foolishly called his friends and began discussing how my genital was mutilated through FGM as if he were having a mental breakdown and could not control himself. I struggled to understand how the topic of FGM was relevant to the situation at hand. In truth, the only time Samuel and I shared real intimacy was when he had nothing. His arrival in America revealed his true nature; he viewed me as his servant. Things worsened when I became a nurse. All he wanted was for me to work and hand over my hard-earned money to him so he could by expensive clothes. He would often say, *"You are my investment, and I must reap my dividends."* After those long night shifts, I had no time for family, leaving me feeling useless. I couldn't fulfill my role as a mother or enjoy being a wife, and I began to regret my nursing career.

The enemy is incredibly cunning. At times, one must learn to wield the very weapons that the enemy has used against them to inflict harm. If you fail to do so, they will persist in using those weapons to torment you. *"However, the very power that led to the collapse of our civilization also paved the way for our future. It granted us the ability to breathe underwater, and thus, we evolved."* (Nuidis Vulko-Aquaman1). Samuel believed he could manipulate my feelings regarding my mother and my past with FGM to sway my decision about my bank account. He confided in his friends that the only way to truly hurt me was to evict my mother from our home. He was also aware of my discomfort in discussing the FGM issue. What he failed to understand is that these actions were patterns he had repeated throughout our marriage. I have witnessed his disrespect towards elderly individuals and those who have supported him along his journey. While I was distressed by the way he treated my mother, it did not compel me to grant him access to my bank account. The FGM practice is something I am not proud to discuss. The enemy will go to great lengths to break you, targeting what is most precious to you or those you least expect. Yet, I urge you to remain steadfast and keep your focus on the Most High God. He is a God who fights every battle on behalf of His children. You will emerge victorious if you understand that *"the weapon for the battle is not physical."* There are many plans in a man's heart; nevertheless, it is the counsel of the Lord that will prevail. Proverbs 19:21.

CHAPTER 18

Now I See Why the Fight Was Tough

As we navigate our struggles, we find that God walks beside us, yet the path ahead often remains shrouded in uncertainty. We engage in battle with courage, faith, and armor, but the ultimate victory may be obscured by a veil of mist. This lack of clarity can be disconcerting. We long to witness the triumph over adversity and the resolution of our hardships. However, it is possible that this very obscurity fortifies our determination. It drives us to fight with steadfast faith, trusting in a grander plan that remains hidden from our view. It compels us to lean on God's strength rather than our own limited perspective. Just as a master sculptor conceals the final masterpiece from the chipping hammer, God encourages us to concentrate on the present task, believing that each strike, each challenge, brings us closer to a magnificent, unforeseen outcome. In the absence of a definitive conclusion, we discover the chance to deepen our faith, surrendering to the mystery with the assurance that God's love serves as the compass guiding us through the struggle.

1st Kings Chapter 13 narrates the story of two prophets: an old prophet and a young prophet. The young prophet, described as a man of God, was sent from Judah to deliver a message to the idolatrous king Jeroboam in Bethel. God fulfilled His promise by enabling the prophet to convey His message and by providing an immediate sign to demonstrate that the young prophet was indeed sent by Him, especially when the king attempted to disrespect him. However, despite performing a miraculous act commanded by God in front of his adversaries, the young prophet was deceived by an 'ungodly' old prophet, leading him to disobey God's command, which ultimately resulted in his death.

This story is a unique example to learn from as believers of our Lord and Savior Jesus Christ. As children of God, we ought to always seek the Lord for guardians rather than just listening to what people say and make decisions based on what we hear. As Matthew Henry put it in his Biblical Commentary on 1 King 13, *"God's people are more in danger of being drawn from their duty by the plausible pretenses of divinity and sanctity than by external inducements; we have therefore need to beware of false prophets, and not believe every spirit."* It is a good thing to know the God you serve for yourself and not only by the preaching you hear or prophecies. There are too many prophets and church leaders in the world today who will come to lead you astray if you allow them to. Sometimes we are easily misled when we act based on what people tell us without seeking God's guidance.

As discussed in previous chapters, my husband's behavior became increasingly unbearable for both me and our children. His arrogant demeanor stripped away my sanity, ultimately impacting my daily performance and interactions at work and within the community. There came a point when I could no longer tolerate the situation; I decided to distance myself from him in hopes that it would encourage a change in his behavior towards me.

Unmasking: A Journey Through Fear to Embrace Reality

The man I once loved and admired, whom I met and struggled alongside in Liberia, had transformed into someone who felt like a character from a horror movie. Our conversations dwindled to nothing, as he demeaned and belittled me daily. After he threw my mother out of our home, I had hoped that this would alleviate his distress and prompt a change in his conduct. Unfortunately, things only worsened.

His actions reaffirmed a statement he had made to me years earlier: *"no money, no love."* One day, I reflected on my situation and thought, *"Why should I sacrifice my connection with my family when he shows no regard for my well-being and continues to make me miserable?"* Consequently, in June 2018, I reached out to our older daughters to inform them of my decision to find a new place to live for the sake of my mental health and to give their father some space. I explained that I would not be taking Ernestine and Louise with me, as they were now adults, but I would be taking Elaine and JoAnn, who were younger and would need assistance with their hair and other preparations for school. Upon hearing my plan, both girls responded, *"No, mammie, we can't stay here with daddy. Do you see how he has been behaving? We're going with you."* Given that the girls were old enough to make their own decisions, I felt I could not force them to stay.

After weeks of searching for a suitable place, I finally found a home near Elaine and JoAnn's school in Lexington, South Carolina. We moved in at the end of June. This decision came after I sought assistance from the head of the Army Chaplains at Fort Jackson. After discussing the issues in our home and requesting his intervention, he arranged for counseling sessions for Samuel and me, emphasizing our privacy since Samuel was pastoring the gospel service at Fort Jackson. He and his wife would conduct the sessions instead of referring us to another chaplain on the base. We began our counseling, but despite multiple visits, the situation continued to deteriorate. Consequently, I decided to prioritize my mental health and take a step back. Nevertheless, to maintain our family's privacy, I continued to take the children to the Fort Jackson Gospel Service where Samuel was pastoring.

While pastoring the Fort Jackson Gospel Service, we connected with a lovely family from the church—a man and his wife. The woman was one of the ministers there, and they treated us with great kindness. She referred to Samuel and me as her children, and the girls as her grandchildren. Occasionally, they would invite us to their home for lunch after service. I held this couple in high regard, particularly admiring the husband for the respect he showed his wife and the care he provided for her. Their genuine love for one another was evident.

Samuel, however, spoke poorly of me to them, revealing that I had moved out of our home. I distinctly remember the man asking me, *"Does your husband see you as his equal or even as his wife?"* His wife then added, *"He mentioned that you grew up in a household with many people, and that the woman you lived with was not married, so you may not understand what it means to have a hus-*

band." Although they posed these questions, they did not disclose that Samuel had informed them of his intention to file for divorce. Instead, the woman encouraged me to return home, saying she had sensed my absence even before Samuel mentioned it. She shared that she had a dream in which the Lord revealed to her that I had moved out, and upon asking Samuel, he confirmed it. She then urged me, *"My daughter, go back home."*

Just two days after our conversation, while browsing the internet, I stumbled upon our home listed for rent. Seeing it online felt surreal. I immediately called the contact number provided on the website to confirm I wasn't dreaming. A woman answered, and I inquired, *"Why is my home posted for rent without my knowledge?"* She apologized and assured me she would take it down immediately. Although she did not disclose who had given her permission to list the house, I chose not to press further. Within 15 minutes, the listing was removed.

I called our church mother to share what had transpired, and she responded, *"This is why I said you should go home."* It turned out that Samuel had received a Permanent Change of Station (PCS) order from the military for Fort Riley in Kansas. He decided to rent out the house since he was leaving South Carolina, without considering the impact on the girls and me.

Sometimes, God reveals signs of impending danger before it occurs, yet we often overlook these warnings due to our distractions and emotions. I received numerous signs from God urging me to reconsider my decision to go to Fort Riley with Samuel, but I allowed myself to be swayed by the opinions of others. When Samuel realized he couldn't rent the house without my approval, he attempted to be more agreeable. He announced to the church that he had been ordered for a Permanent Change of Station (PCS) to Fort Riley, Kansas, in January 2019, and that he would be moving with his family.

A few weeks before Samuel's relocation, our church mother invited us to her home on a Sunday evening for a discussion. This time, it was just me and the girls. She took me aside to share the challenges she and her husband faced in their marriage, encouraging me to consider moving back home. Witnessing their peaceful and romantic relationship, along with hearing their struggles, inspired me to believe that my own marriage could improve. I thought to myself, *"If they can endure and thrive, so can we."* Thus, I made the decision to move back home, despite the girls' discontent with my choice.

After relocating, we began planning for our move to Kansas, even though we had a few months before the actual date. During this planning phase, Samuel made a second trip to South Africa. I didn't perceive any ulterior motives behind his visit; I believed he was attending a church conference to campaign for a bishop position. However, he also decided to take a vacation to South Africa before starting his new assignment. Before his departure, he suddenly became unusually affectionate, declaring, *"I don't want to live without my family anymore; we all need to move to Kansas."* I tried to persuade him to let the girls and me stay behind to finish the school term, planning to join him in the summer, but he was adamant.

Ernestine and Louise did not accompany us to Kansas, as they were both in college at the time. Samuel engaged a leasing company to put our house back on the market since we were relocating. Our home seemed lively again, as Samuel was no longer easily irritated or angry. However, our two older daughters were skeptical. They remarked, *"Mammie, the change in Daddy's behavior in such a short time feels too good to be true. He was too high-strung to change this quickly."* I reassured them, saying, *"People can change. Perhaps he genuinely wants a peaceful family life, especially with the upcoming relocation."* Yet, their concerns proved valid, as after Samuel and I signed the lease for our home, his behavior began to shift once more.

In January 2019, Samuel left for his assignment at Fort Riley. Shortly thereafter, the military arrived to empty our house, transporting our belongings to Kansas. We were left with only a few items to use until we settled into our new home. The night before our trip, we packed the remainder of our possessions into my 2012 Dodge Caravan. The two little girls were unhappy about leaving their school, especially Elaine, but they had no choice. Daddy wanted us to accompany him, and I wanted to be with my husband as well. We departed in the van around 6:30 AM, heading for Fort Riley, Kansas, a journey that would take a little over 17 hours. I decided to drive most of the distance before taking a break for the night.

We drove all day, yet Samuel did not call to check on us; his silence spoke volumes. Whenever he traveled this same route, I would stay on the phone, checking in on him regularly. After a day and a half of driving, we arrived at Fort Riley on the evening of February 3, 2019. However, upon reaching the house, we found it locked, and Samuel was not home. I called to inform him of our arrival, and after an hour of waiting, he sent someone with the key to let us in. Two hours later, he came home, his face devoid of emotion. When I asked why he hadn't checked on us during our journey, he replied, "*You didn't call me either. If you wanted me to know what was happening with you and the girls, you should have called.*" Not wanting to engage in an argument, I remained silent. His response revealed that he had not changed since our time in South Carolina. I was determined not to reopen old wounds; I simply wanted us to focus on our family and resolve our issues for a better life together. For a brief moment, it seemed like our relationship was improving. However, just as I began to feel hopeful, Samuel took another trip to South Africa. Upon his return, things seemed fine at first. He brought back jewelry and bags for me to sell, but soon after, his demeanor shifted. He became easily irritated and angered once again.

I did not fully grasp the situation until I learned that Samuel had informed our church mother of his intention to get a divorce. At that moment, I was unaware of his plans when she advised me, "Just go and be a wife." After leaving South Carolina, she continued to call our daughter, inquiring whether we were still together. Eventually, she told the girl, *"Your father said he was going to divorce."* I believe her encouragement for me to support my husband was well-intentioned, especially considering her own happy and successful marriage. However, knowing Samuel's plan to divorce while still urging me to *"just go and be a wife"* feels deceptive. This resonates with Matthew Henry's commentary, which states, *"Believers are most in danger of being drawn from their duty by the plausible pretenses of holiness."*

I accepted the advice of my church mother and several other church members, following my husband on his military assignment and sacrificing my own career in the process. Had she not mentioned his intentions to our daughter, I would have remained oblivious to Samuel's plans for divorce when he asked me to accompany him. I suspect he researched divorce laws in Kansas before persuading me to move with him, as obtaining a divorce in South Carolina is not a quick process; the couple must be separated for at least one year. Furthermore, Samuel did not want our children and me present in the South Carolina home when he filed for divorce, as our presence would have significantly increased the likelihood of retaining the home. Consequently, he manipulated me into relocating with him, and this manipulation was further supported by someone I deeply respected.

The story of the young prophet in 1 Kings chapter 13 serves as a poignant reminder of the dangers of misplaced trust. This prophet did not lack faith in God; rather, he mistakenly placed his confidence in the perceived wisdom and experience of an older prophet. He believed that the age gap conferred greater insight and understanding to the older man. However, he failed to recognize that when God calls us, He equips us for the mission ahead, as illustrated in Exodus 4:11-12 and Hebrews 13:21.

Many Christians fall into similar traps, believing that God will reveal profound truths about them through others rather than directly to them. This can lead to deep disappointment, especially when we realize that God is indeed speaking to us about our circumstances, yet we choose to ignore His warnings. As believers, we must not second-guess ourselves when we clearly hear the voice of God and recognize it as His.

When we engage with scripture and grasp God's instructions through His word, it is imperative that we act upon what He says. Furthermore, when God communicates with us, it is always for our benefit. Ignoring His guidance often leads to negative consequences.

It is also unwise for Christians to share what God has revealed to them about their own lives with others. Doing so can expose us to envy, jealousy, and manipulation, leading us to question whether we truly heard from God. As Matthew Henry notes in his commentary on 1 Kings 13, the man of God initially resisted the king's invitation, despite the promise of a reward. Yet, he was ultimately persuaded by the older prophet to return and dine in Bethel, contrary to God's command.

The dialogue between the old and young prophet, beginning in 1 Kings 13:15, highlights the young prophet's awareness of God's instruction not to eat or drink in Bethel. His inexperience led him to disclose God's directives to the old prophet, who then used this information to lead him astray. Being overly accommodating to the enemy can be detrimental to achieving victory in spiritual battles.

Reflecting on my experiences, I now understand why the battle was so difficult to win. I followed misguided advice, and perhaps I should have remained silent, continuing to fight while trusting in the restorative power of God. The Devil thrives on spectacle, roaring and tempting with grand proclamations, reveling in the chaos he creates. Yet, often, the most potent weapon against him is quiet effectiveness. It is the unwavering resolve that burns silently within us, the steadfast focus that allows us, as children of God, to see through his illusions. We do not need a booming voice or a flashy display of power to achieve victory; we simply need to act with purpose, countering his bluster with calculated moves.

Each temptation we deflect, each task we complete that chips away at the enemy's grip, is a quietly earned victory. In the midst of a fight, not everyone stands as our ally. The devil, or enemy, wears many disguises. He may rage and gnash his teeth, but our quiet effectiveness reveals him for the fraud he truly is. It demonstrates that true strength lies not in empty showmanship, but in the unwavering spirit that perseveres. In the face of the enemy's storm, we become an immovable mountain, the calm in the eye of the hurricane. As he witnesses his grand designs crumble under the weight of our quiet defiance, we will see a flicker of fear in his eyes. After all, a silent enemy, one who cannot be swayed or intimidated, is the Devil's greatest nightmare. Looking back now, all I can say is, *'WOW!'*

CHAPTER 19

Why Did I Stay?

The choice to remain in an abusive marriage is a multifaceted issue, shaped by psychological factors and religious beliefs. Abusers often excel at isolating their victims, gradually undermining their self-esteem and instilling a sense of learned helplessness. This, combined with the fear of escalating violence or threats to children, can leave women like me feeling trapped. Samue Siebo was a master of it all. Furthermore, some women may cling to the hope that they can *'fix'* their partner or downplay the abuse as a coping mechanism for their trauma. At one point, I believed I could have changed my ex-husband's abusive behavior, as he had essentially raised himself, being born out of wedlock. He did not grow up in a household with both a husband and a wife, and he had to leave his mother at a young age to fend for himself. In contrast, I was raised in a polygamous home with both parents present, as well as in a foster family where both parents were also involved. Samuel Siebo, however, never experienced such stability and therefore did not appreciate the value of a committed marital relationship. I remained in the marriage due to a multitude of factors.

The intricate interplay of psychological factors often ensnares many women in abusive marriages. Fear stands out as a predominant factor, as abusers frequently isolate their victims, rendering the act of leaving both perilous and isolating. Trauma bonding—a connection forged through intermittent cycles of abuse and affection—fosters a confusing sense of loyalty. Abusive partners systematically undermine self-esteem, leading victims to doubt their own perceptions and self-worth. Additionally, the hope for change, the desire to protect children, and societal pressures to maintain a marriage can further complicate the situation. This toxic combination of fear, manipulation, and distorted self-perception makes the decision to leave exceedingly challenging.

Religion can complicate the situation further. Certain interpretations highlight the sanctity of marriage and regard divorce as a sin, which can leave women feeling overwhelming guilt or shame when contemplating separation. Doctrines that promote male dominance may also play a role, leading women to doubt their right to challenge their husband's behavior.

It is crucial to recognize that religion can serve as a source of strength for individuals in abusive marriages or romantic relationships. Many faiths denounce abuse and provide support systems to assist women in escaping such situations. Ultimately, the choice to leave lies with the individual, and it is essential to consider both psychological and religious influences when navigating the journey toward safety and healing.

One late morning on January 9, 2024, while sitting

UNMASKING: A JOURNEY THROUGH FEAR TO EMBRACE REALITY

at work I received a text message from Louise who seemed to have something weighing on her mind:

> She wrote, *"Hey, mommy, are you working today?"*
> "Yes, why?" I asked.
> *"Ok nothing much, I'll call you later tonight when you're done with work and before prayer time,"* she said.
> I asked, *"I'm about to take my break now. Do you want to talk?"*
> *"No, let's talk when you're home,"* she replied.
> *"Ok,"* I responded.

That night, after arriving home, I took a shower and, before prayer time, called Louise as she had suggested. At some point, Louise and I were engaged in virtual prayers before bed, despite the distance between us—she in New York and I in Georgia. *"Hey Louise, are you ready to talk now?"* I inquired. After a brief pause, she replied, *"Oh no, Mommy, I don't want to talk again."* Her response piqued my curiosity. *"Why not?"* I pressed. *"I'm okay now,"* she said, her tone subdued. I was eager to understand what had prompted her to want to talk earlier but not now. I continued to encourage her, and eventually, she relented, saying, *"Okay, fine, I will talk."*

She began to tell me, *"You know mommy, I was in my therapy session today and I don't remember how we got here but our family issues came up, and I was wondering how you stayed in that abusive marriage and felt that it was ok. What is your view on marriage? How did you see yourself in that marriage? When I think about all that you went through in your marriage and how it ended up with you, I feel so bad for you. You sacrificed your happiness for an abusive marriage that you would be determined to stay in all your life if your husband had not ended up divorcing you. You kept telling us, I want to keep the family together, and I told you that you were not helping us. You never had time with us, especially Elaine and JoAnn. All you did was work, and work. Elaine and JoAnn practically grew up with daddy, that's why they are so hurt by the divorce, since their father abandoned them as well."* She paused for a while and then continued.

"Even after what your husband did to Ernestine, my sister, and his own daughter, you heard it, and you were still in that kind of marriage. Isn't what he did to Ernestine a sin, having sex with his own child? But you are totally against same sex relationships or gay and lesbian and abortion. But then you accepted to be with a man who raped his own daughter, even though sin is sin. I understand Ernestine told us what he did to her after the fact, and you didn't know all the details surrounding what she went through but you stayed there. Why would you want to be married to a man who molested his own daughter in the first place? This is a man who speaks ill of you and discusses you with his friends and his girlfriends. Is it because he's good looking? I mean you were the one making the money so why were you with this man that had no respect

for you? It is sad mommy. You could have avoided this marriage in the first place. The man was not honest with you from the beginning. What made you think he would have been honest later? There has to be some other reason for staying in that marriage other than not wanting a divorce. Anyway, we can't continue to dwell on the past, but I hope that your next decision will be better. I think you can still have a better marriage life. I also pray that daddy repents of his sins and his evil ways so he can have peace of mind." When she was done speaking, I was completely dumbfounded. It was like I was hit with a jackhammer in my stomach.

This conversation with Louise revealed a bitter truth that I had not anticipated. Her strong stance caught me off guard, but it ultimately served as an eye-opener. The truth can be painful, yet those who are willing to change and do what is right will embrace this discomfort to enhance their lives and behaviors. I was unaware of my own shortcomings regarding sin until after our discussion. It took the perspective of my child, whom I brought into this world, to illuminate this reality for me. I have come to understand that my views on gays, lesbians, and abortion issues are fundamentally contradictory to the essence of Christianity. Jesus did not instruct us to fixate on a single aspect of the Bible or to point fingers at our neighbors or those with whom we disagree. As it is clearly written in the Bible, *"Don't you realize that those who do wrong will not inherit the Kingdom of God? Don't fool yourselves. Those who indulge in sexual sin, or who worship idols, or commit adultery, or are male prostitutes, or practice homosexuality, or are thieves, or greedy people, or drunkards, or are abusive, or cheat people—none of these will inherit the Kingdom of God."* 1Corinthians 6:9-10(NLT). While I am not insinuating that the church endorse gay marriage or vilify it, but rather, the church should preach and teach the liberating words of God which is against all sins.

One cannot serve God with half-heartedness and expect to succeed. He desires our honesty in our walk with Him, and in return, He will guide us toward paths that honor His name. Regardless of the situation you find yourself in, trust in the Lord, heed His voice, and seek His guidance.

I spent 21 years in an abusive marriage, concealing lies as the wife of a pastor, all in the name of protecting my marriage. I clung to the scripture that states God hates divorce, yet my husband would stand in the pulpit and speak falsehoods, to which I would acquiesce. One of the reasons was that I feared leaving a marriage I believed had accumulated too much wealth for me to abandon. People remain in relationships or organizations for various reasons. However, I urge you to eliminate anything that interferes with your relationship with God. When you trust God enough to distance yourself from those obstacles that the enemy uses to hinder you, He will reveal His presence and power in your life.

Unmasking: A Journey Through Fear to Embrace Reality

Genesis chapter 26 narrates the story of Isaac's experiences in the land of the Philistines, where God blessed the work of his hands. This divine favor led to envy among the Philistines, who ultimately drove him away. Rather than retaliating, Isaac chose to leave peacefully. The Bible recounts that he faced significant opposition, prompting him to name two of his wells Esek and Sitnah, which signify contention and hatred. Whenever the Philistines grew dissatisfied with the wells he dug, Isaac moved on until he discovered a well in a place free from strife, which he named Rehoboth, meaning enlargement, space, or enough room. The Scriptures affirm that God blessed Isaac abundantly. At times, God permits us to endure trials to gauge our closeness to Him and the depth of our trust. In moments of despair, when we feel utterly defeated, God reveals His strength on our behalf. As Matthew Henry eloquently states in his Bible Commentary, "When men are false and unkind, God remains faithful and gracious; His timing to manifest this is often when we are most let down by others." God will never shortchange you compared to what your adversaries have taken. Steer clear of strife and discontent, and embrace your Rehoboth blessings.

JENNIFER'S PHOTO BURSTS
Liberia
Gipo

South Carolina

South Carolina

Kansas

CH (CPT) SAMUEL D. SIEBO FOR BISHOP AMEC 2020

CH (CPT) SAMUEL D. SIEBO FOR BISHOP AMEC 2020
SCHOOL & HOSPITAL PROJECT-LIBERIA

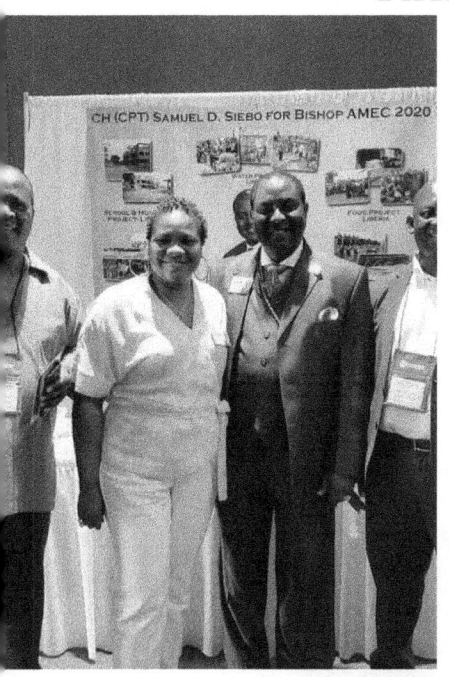

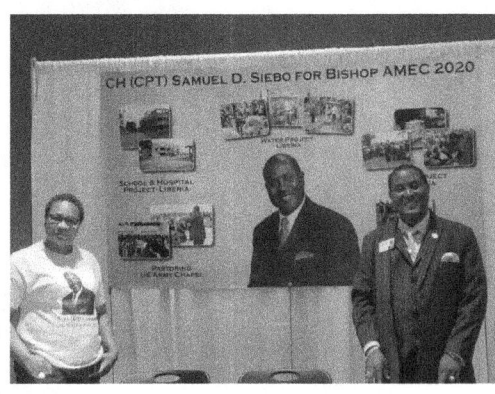

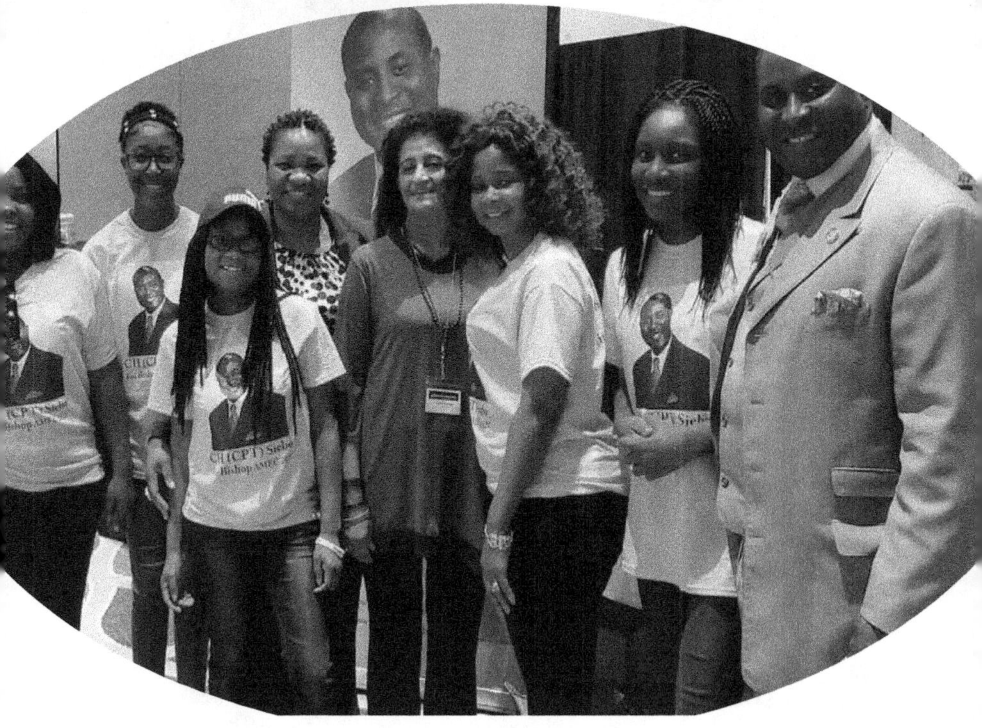

My Random Photo Bursts

Random Photo Bursts

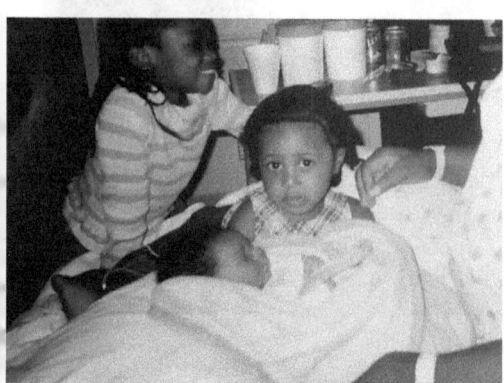

THE END

CREDITS

Designed by Clarke Publishing Communications & BPO, Inc.
(AKA, Clarke Publishing)
Jacket design by Albert Kizuo
Jacket Photo supplied by Jennifer Yah Legay (Jenniferlegay.com)

At Clarke Publishing, we bring your dreams to life!

Author's Bio

Jennifer is a remarkable woman of faith who has held numerous leadership roles within her church and community. She served as the Director of the Young People's Division (YPD) of the AME Church in Liberia for four years and was the President of the Women's Missionary Society (WMS) at Greene Memorial AME Church in Barnesville, Liberia for eight years. Additionally, she was a member of the Board of Directors for the 14th Episcopal District of the AME Church. Jennifer firmly believes in the power of prayer and took the initiative to organize the Prayer Warrior Team at Greene Memorial AMEC.

With a deep passion for community growth and development, Jennifer founded and named her community, the Bethel Hill Community, in Barnesville, Liberia. She served as its first president from 2001 until December 2004, when she relocated to the United States. During her presidency, she actively participated in seminars, workshops, and training sessions organized by the United States Agency for International Development (USAID), the United Nations Development Program (UNDP), and other developmental agencies to secure assistance for her community. Today, Bethel Hill Community stands as one of the most prominent and developed communities in the Township of Barnesville.

Professionally, Jennifer is a Board Certified Family Nurse Practitioner. She graduated from East Tennessee State University in Johnson City, Tennessee, earning her Bachelor of Science in Nursing (BSN) in May 2011 and her Master of Science in Nursing (MSN) with a concentration in Family Medicine in December 2016. Jennifer currently lives in Georgia with her daughters.

www.ingramcontent.com/pod-product-compliance
Lightning Source LLC
Chambersburg PA
CBHW060029180426
43196CB00044B/2044